The Authorities

Powerful Wisdom from Leaders in the Field

YAVUZ ALTUN

Award Winning Author

AuthoritiesPress

Copyright © 2019 Authorities Press

ISBN: 978-1-07672-437-3

Publisher
Authorities Press
Markham, ON
Canada

Printed in the United States, Canada, and the United Kingdom.

FOREWORD

Experts are to be admired for their knowledge, but they often remain unrecognized by the general public because they save their information and insights for paying customers and clients. There are many experts in a given field, but their impact is limited to the handful of people with whom they work.

Unlike experts, authorities share their knowledge and expertise far more broadly, so they make a big impact on the world. Authorities become known and admired as leading experts and, as such, typically do very well economically and professionally. Most authorities are also mature enough to know that part of the joy of monetary success is the accompanying moral and spiritual obligation to give back.

Many people want to learn and work with well-respected and generous authorities, but don't always know where to find them. They may be known to their peers, or within a specific community, but have not had the opportunity to reach a wider audience. At one time, they might have submitted a proposal to the For Dummies or Chicken Soup for the Soul series of books, but it's now almost impossible to get accepted as a new author in such branded book series.

It is more than fitting that Raymond Aaron, an internationally known and respected authority in his own right, would be the one to recognize the need for a new venue in which authorities could share their considerable knowledge with readers everywhere. As the only author ever to be included in both of the book series mentioned above, Raymond has had the opportunity to give back and he understands how crucial it is for authorities to have a platform from which to share their expertise.

I

I have known and worked with Raymond for a number of years and consider him a valued friend and talented coach. He knows how to spot talented and knowledgeable people and he desires to see them prosper. Over the years, success coaching and speaking engagements around the world have made it possible for Raymond to meet many of these talented authorities. He recognizes and relates to their passion and enthusiasm for what they do, as well as their desire to share what they know. He tells me that's why he created this new nonfiction branded book series, The Authorities.

Dr. Nido Qubein
President, High Point University

TABLE OF CONTENTS

INTRODUCTION

This book introduces you to *The Authorities* — individuals who have distinguished themselves in life and in business. Authorities make a big impact on the world. Authorities are leaders in their chosen fields. Authorities typically do very well financially, and are evolved enough to know that part of the joy of monetary success is the accompanying social, moral and spiritual obligation to give back.

Authorities are not just outstanding. They are also *known* to be outstanding.

This additional element begins to explain the difference between two strategic business and life concepts — one that seems great, but isn't, and the other that fills in the essential missing gap of the first.

The first concept is "the expert."

What is an expert? The real definition is …

EXPERT: *a person who knows stuff*

People who have attained a very senior academic degree (like a PhD or an MD) definitely know stuff. People who read voraciously and retain what they read definitely know stuff. Unfortunately, just because you know stuff does not mean that anyone respects the fact that you do. Even though some experts are successful, alas, most are not — because knowing stuff is not enough.

Well, then, what is the missing piece?

What the expert lacks, "the authority" has. The authority both knows stuff and is *known* to know stuff. So, more simply …

AUTHORITY: *a person who is known as an expert*

The difference is not subtle. The difference is not merely semantic. The difference is enormous.

When it comes to this subject, there are actually three categories in which people fall:

- People who don't know much and are unsuccessful in life and in business. Most people fall in this category.

- People who know stuff, but still don't leave much of a footprint in the world. There are a lot of people like this.

- Experts who are also *known* as experts become authorities and authorities are always wondrously successful. Authorities are able to contribute more to humanity through both their chosen work and their giving back.

This book is about the highest category, *The Authorities* — people who have reached the peak in their field and are known as such.

You will definitely know some of *The Authorities* in this book, especially since there are some world-famous ones. Others are just as exceptional, but you may not yet know about them. Let me introduce you to Yavuz Altun, our featured author. Yavuz Altun was born in a small beautiful city in 'Van' close to the biggest Lake in Turkey. He went to Istanbul after primary school to help in his family's food wholesale business.

Continuing his education, Yavuz graduated with an Industrial Engineering from Eastern Mediterranean University, a MBA from Thames Valley University and a Masters in Marketing from Bilgi University. He attended a program for Business Dynamics, Understanding and Solving Complex Business Problems at the Massachusetts Institute of Technology (MIT)—Sloan School of Management. He also graduated from the Harvard Business School

Program for Leadership Development (equivalent to an Executive MBA). He even attended, with Chairman of Turkcell Ahmet Akça and Turkish Foreign Minister Mevlüt Çavuşoğlu, the Global Forum of the United Nations Alliance of Civilizations (UNAOC) to contribute to the peace process in the world in United Nations headquarters in New York.

He has been the CEO at the Happy Center Supermarket Chain (135 stores in 5 different cities) for more than 18 years and is also the Chairman at happy.com.tr, an online shopping platform which serves 81 cities around Turkey. His company exports fast moving consumer goods in more than 30 countries. Yavuz is also a professional public speaker who has international speaking engagements in Europe, the UK, North America and Asia to leading universities, chambers of commerce, business groups and nonprofit organizations. And he is a serial Entrepreneur who has several startup companies such as **www.restajet.com** and **www.dotsonnet.net**. Having experience in business process transformation and innovation in Grocery Retailing in the Supermarket Industry for more than 20 years, Yavuz has a successful background regarding defining business strategies and leading global transformation know how transfer. He's passionate about innovation and new technologies, developed Erp and digital platforms where related functions generated for efficient and effective business units in his company.

He has been elected to the following current Organizations: Istanbul Chamber of Commerce Committee Member and Assembly Member that represents 420,000 companies; Member of the Board of Directors at Turkey's EU Expert Economic Development Foundation Iktisadi Kalkınma Vakfı (IKV) Organization specializing in the EU and Turkey-EU relations since 1965; Istanbul Chamber of Commerce Education and Social Services foundation General Assembly Member; Esenyurt Tax Office Appreciation Commission Member; Delegate of Exporters Union that represents 70,000 Turkish Exporters; Istanbul Chamber of Commerce Retail Trade Vice-

Chairman; and Member of the Board of Directors Turkey Cereals Pulses Oil Seeds and Products Exporters Union. He is also Member of the Board of Directors Turkish Cyprus (Turkish Republic of Northern Cyprus) Chamber of Commerce which represents to develop trade between two countries.

Yavuz is an engineer and father of four kids.

WOW! Enjoy his chapter, *Exponential Growth Strategy*, and get in line for the book by the same name. Yavuz will not steer you in the wrong direction.

They are *The Authorities*. Learn from them. Connect with them. Let them uplift you. Learning from them and working with them is the secret ingredient for success which may well allow you to rise to the level of Authority soon.

To be considered for inclusion in a subsequent edition of *The Authorities*, register to attend a future event at www.aaron.com/events where you will be interviewed and considered.

Exponential Growth Strategy

The 9 P System

YAVUZ ALTUN

There are 9 Ps in the *Exponential Growth Strategy* and this Authorities chapter deals with the very first one – Power. If you would like more information, please contact me atyavuzaltun@happy.com.tr and I will be happy to explain each one personally to you in more detail.

#1 POWER

True power isn't about force, position, or authority. It's about influence.

On the Way to Transformation

When you close your eyes, you can see more of what you are imagining. So, keeping your eyes closed, allow yourself to dream and imagine how you'll achieve your dream. This activity has the potential to break barriers within you, so do it again and again to find your purpose and your biggest 'why' (e.g. Why do you want to pursue this dream?).

However, when you chase a dream, you need to be aware that it always, always creates change. It may also create growth, but your success journey will focus on change—from self-development to the corporate level of any organizations you're involved with—rather than on growth. Why? Well, how you respond to change is everything. Think of it in terms of discovery and action. In the end it creates knowledge, and knowledge is power.

Sears, Nokia, Kodak, Kmart, ToysRus and Blockbuster all have similar stories of how they responded to growth rather than to market changes. Edward Abbey said, "Growth for the sake of growth is the ideology of the cancer cell." So, companies that have a strategy for responding to growth rather than change experience failure in their organization like a cancer cell destroying the body. This is also true regarding each individual who responds to or focuses on growth rather than change.

It's all about doing and acting instead of knowing how to do and act.

It's about changing constantly and surviving. When everybody looks at the ball, you need to look at the field. When everybody looks at the ball, you need to look where the ball could be going.

It's not about thinking inside the box or thinking outside the box or thinking there is no box. If there's nothing, you can start to think from zero.

Consciousness prefers knowledge; he who doesn't know anything also doesn't know himself because knowing begins with knowing what you know. Yukio Mishima describes this very well:

What transforms this world is — knowledge. Do you see what I mean? Nothing else can change anything in this world. Knowledge alone is capable of transforming the world, while at the same time leaving it exactly as it is. When you look at the world with knowledge, you realize that things are unchangeable and at the same time are constantly being transformed.

—Yukio Mishima

Knowing

I was watching a Steve Jobs speech until midnight on the 4th of October, 2011. When I woke up, I watched the news and learned that he had lost his life. I realized that I had watched Steve's last appearance. I was shocked and very upset. You see, when I was 17, I read a quote that went something like, "If you live each day as if it were your last, someday you'll most certainly be right." It made an impression on me and since then, for the past 33 years, I have looked in the mirror every morning and asked myself, "If today were the last day of my life, would I want to do what I'm about to do today." But when I had a chance, I didn't go to see Steve Jobs. I still remember that night like today. It reaffirmed what I had set out to do, and I made a decision not to make that mistake again. I experienced change and moved closer to my destiny.

Don't forget that what you're looking for is also looking for you. It's called the Law of Attraction: what you put out into the universe will attract the same. Hence, the quality of your life is the quality of the choices you make. Change your choices, especially your significant choices. For example, anyone can be great when his heart holds the intention to serve. The world is better with givers than it is with takers. The secret to purpose is its connection with purity.

The time is now to take full charge of your life. It's all about changing based on belief and making a decision. When your purpose is bigger, then your obstacles become smaller and smaller. Vision creates the possibility to see what you have been unable to see. Where you are today isn't where you end up. Life is never stuck; we just feel stuck. We need to get in touch with our childhood dream. Children have no limitations when it comes to dreaming.

We all are gifted but some people never try to open their gifts, they're too busy comparing themselves with others. You need to stop doubting and stop comparing your gifts with others. Others can't see what you're able to see.

Without purpose it isn't possible to integrate and improve. We need to change things to make things happen. We don't know which day will be the last day of our life. It's not where we start, it's where we are going. Lets listen to Yunus ...

> *Knowledge should mean a full grasp of knowledge:*
> *Knowledge means to know yourself, heart and soul.*
> *If you have failed to understand yourself,*
> *Then all of your reading has missed its call.*
>
> *What is the purpose of reading those books?*
> *So that Man can know the All-Powerful.*
> *If you have read, but failed to understand,*
> *Then your efforts are just a barren toil.*
>
> *Don't boast of reading, mastering science*
> *Or of all your prayers and obeisance.*
> *If you don't identify Man,*
> *All your learning is of no use at all.*

The true meaning of the four holy books
Is found in the alphabet's first letter.
You talk about that first letter, preacher;
What is the meaning of that-could you tell?

Yunus Emre says to you, Pharisee,
Make the holy pilgrimage if need be
A hundred times-but if you ask me,
The visit to a heart is best of all.

—Yunus Emre

Yes, your transformation will be hard. Yes, you will feel frightened, messed up and knocked down. Yes, you'll want to stop. Yes, it's the best work you'll ever do.

—Robin Sharma

When you fight yourself to discover the real you, there is only one winner.

—Stephen Richards

If you live each day as if it were your last, how enormous could the impact for your decisions and your freedom be? Those looking for transformation always look for "What's missing". Using Power on the way to transformation always creates commitment and is highly motivating, energizing and empowering. If you look at book titles like *Think and Grow Rich, The 7 Habits of Highly Effective People: Powerful Lessons in Personal Change, Awaken the Giant Within, The Leader Who Had No Title: A Modern Fable on Real Success in Business and in Life, Purple Cow: Transform Your Business by Being Remarkable, How to Win Friends & Influence People, You are a Badass: How to Stop Doubting Your Greatness* and *Start Living an Awesome Life, Daring Greatly: How the Courage to Be Vulnerable Transforms the Way We Live, Love, Parent, and Lead, and Practicing the Power of Now,* all of them are about motivating you to get better and better. How can you be systemizing the way you've modeled others on the way to transformation?

Let's look at story from the Rumi …

> *Some Hindus have an elephant to show.*
> *No one here has ever seen an elephant.*
> *They bring it at night to a dark room.*
> *One by one, we go in the dark and come out*
> *saying how we experience the animal.*
>
> *One of us happens to touch the trunk.*
> *A water-pipe kind of creature.*
> *Another, the ear. A strong, always moving*
> *back and forth, fan-animal. Another, the leg.*
> *I find it still, like a column on a temple.*
>
> *Another touches the curved back.*
> *A leathery throne. Another, the cleverest,*
> *feels the tusk. A rounded sword made of porcelain.*
> *He is proud of his description.*
>
> *Each of us touches one place*
> *and understands the whole in that way.*
> *The palm and the fingers feeling in the dark*
> *are how the senses explore the reality of the elephant.*
> *If each of us held a candle there,*
> *and if we went in together, we could see it.*
>
> —Rumi, A Year with Rumi

If you know something that others do not know, then you have a very big advantage. Francis Bacon's statement, "knowledge is power" surely is true. If you have knowledge and you don't convert this knowledge to action, then there is no power anymore. After Francis Bacon, other self-development gurus said "action is the source of power". Again, it's true. Yes, you convert the knowledge to action, but you need more stability to get success. Look at Aristotle, who said, "We are what we repeatedly do. Excellence, then, is not an act, but a habit." The idea if to convert knowledge into action and action into habit. Just worry for yourself when building a habit—focus on what you want to achieve and make it part of your routine. Keep what you want to make a habit and go on to better and better things. The same goes for achieving excellence within an organization; habits are the basis of what we continue to do. It's not just an act. It's a habit we try to keep doing day-in and day-out; it's how we live and organize our lives.

I am the drop that contains the ocean.
—Yunus Emre

Change starts in your thoughts.
—Anonymous

We are all butterflies. Earth is our chrysalis.
—LeeAnn Taylor

Love and Mercy

Lovers find secret places inside this violent world where they make transactions with beauty.
—Rumi

(This is the ultimate love from Rumi.)

I choose to love you in silence…
For in silence I find no rejection,
I choose to love you in loneliness…
For in loneliness no one owns you but me,
I choose to adore you from a distance…
For distance will shield me from pain,
I choose to kiss you in the wind…
For the wind is gentler than my lips,
I choose to hold you in my dreams…
For in my dreams, you have no end.

—Rumi

Thirsty

OOnce upon a time, Rose meets with Water and they become friends. The first priority is friendship. During this time, they get to know each other. But then Rose falls in love with Water. And from that moment, all doors were opened, and the fragrances around them were sweet.

She says: "Dear Water, I have changed so much now that I love you. I open my petals, and I smell the fragrance, just because I love you."

It will happen that Water will begin to feel something, and he believes that he is in love with Rose. But as time moves on Water shows even less for the old Rose.

Rose thinks, "I do not think he likes me anymore."

Because his disinterest has begun to upset her, one day Rose says to Water, "Do you know I love you so much?"

Water replies, "I love you too."

Time passes and Rose again says, "I love you."

Water says in a plain expression, "Me too."

But Rose cannot feel this so-called love of his. This routine gets longer and longer.

"I love you very much," he says. But now he's so far gone that Rose can't smell that good smell.

"You know, I still love you very much," he says in tears.

Water turns to her and says with the most ironic and unconcerned utterance he knows, "She is too sick to say I love you too."

Day comes and Rose falls to the beds. Rose is very sick as her color fades and she lies yellowing in the bed. The water waits, loving her so much and loving her every chance.

The last time Rose barely turns her head and says to Water, "Do you know I really love you, and I love you as much as you do not know?"

Grieving, Water, as a last resort, calls a doctor.

"What is the problem?" he asks the doctor.

The doctor examines Rose, then he smiles. After the examination, he says, "The condition of the patient is despairing, nothing will come anymore."

Water wonders what disease is causing the death. He asks the doctor, "What is wrong with my beloved friend? I do not know if she has a sickness, as I have not paid any attention to her."

Doctor says, "Dear friend, this Rose is only thirsty. Death is for you, Water."

Let's ask for a moment, do you know how many times you've become thirsty? How many times have you been dissappointed? Who around you might also be thirsty, without you being aware? Your eyes are open and you think your heart is open, but you aren't aware of them. Without love what you do is a total misconception and you have an unexamined life. You need to see that the door is always open for you, otherwise you stay in prison. The water never feared the fire. Don't wait any longer. Let the sea be you. Dive in the ocean, make your last journey from this strange world. There is no more separation of you and your home.

God created your wings not to be dormant. You're alive, and you must try more to use your wings.

Your light helps you to learn how to love.

Your beauty helps you to learn to stop worrying.

Think who created you and that he'll open his hands if you want to be held.

Everyone Say "Love Yourself."

There's no meaning to life without love for ourselves. Johnny Weir said, "Love myself, I do. Not everything, but I love the good as well as the bad. I love my crazy lifestyle, and I love my hard discipline. I love my freedom of speech and the way my eyes get dark when I'm tired. I love that I have learned to trust people with my heart, even if it will get broken. I am proud of everything that I am and will become."

The opposite side of love is a feeling of rejection. This comes from childhood. When you were little, you were shaped by your environment. You need to reflect back and learn things that you wanted to learn; you need to focus on your dreams. You need to be grateful for being yourself. Because, not only did you learn about who you are, but you also learned what you could be able to do. Sure, you are alone in whatever it is you're facing. We're all born alone, live alone and we'll die alone. So, be in a relationship with your inner self. It's very important to be happy spending time with yourself. If you enjoy spending time with yourself, people will ultimately enjoy spending time with you. Sometimes, talk to yourself. Joke and laugh with yourself. It's very healthy to have a "relationship with yourself". And in order for you to have a good relationship with yourself you have to accept yourself, including the good and the not so good, the beautiful and the not so beautiful. If you want to be in a relationship with another person, you have to love your relationship with yourself first. Love yourself first before loving someone else. You have to love yourself in order to love and accept another person. If you don't get to know yourself and learn how to love and accept yourself how will you get to know anyone else?

Let's listen to Yunus on the way of Love …

Your love has wrested me away from me,
You're the one I need, you're the one I crave.
Day and night I burn, gripped by agony,
You're the one I need, you're the one I crave.
I find no great joy in being alive,

If I cease to exist, I would not grieve,
The only solace I have is your love,
You're the one I need, you're the one I crave.
Lovers yearn for you, but your love slays them,
At the bottom of the sea it lays them,
It has God's images-it displays them;
You're the one I need, you're the one I crave.
Let me drink the wine of love sip by sip,
Like Mecnun, live in the hills in hardship,
Day and night, care for you holds me in its grip,
You're the one I need, you're the one I crave.
Even if, at the end, they make me die
And scatter my ashes up to the sky,
My pit would break into this outcry:
You're the one I need, you're the one I crave.
"Yunus Emre the mystic" is my name,
Each passing day fans and rouses my flame,
What I desire in both worlds in the same:
You're the one I need,
you're the one I crave.

—Yunus Emre

Doing

Socrates declared that the unexamined life was not worth living. Asked to sum up what all philosophical commandments could be reduced to, he replied: *"Know yourself."* Self-knowledge offers a route to greater power, consciousness, joy and fulfillment. Self-knowledge is the formulation of what we do; our life choices, commitment and expectations.

Art has the ability to change minds. Passion is what changes the world. When both collide, it's as powerful as a bomb. Art isn't pretty and poised fluff. Art is brutal and snarling. Artists growl. This is the roar of change that beats within them.

—A.H. Scott

Mankind has evolved into creatures whose minds are divided into the largely logical conscious, and more emotional subconscious, mind. The reason for this division is frequency. You simply couldn't cope if everything you experienced had to be filtered through the conscious mind.

The less you know, the more you will be known
The less you want, the more you will have
The less you are, the more you will be

—Vivian Amis, I Am: The Key to Manifesting

The transformation needs high motivation to connect with a deeper sense of purpose and creating value. Think about Starbucks, Netflix, Amazon, Lego, and Apple: It's not just about innovation or developing new products. Rather, it's about enabling the joy of the user experience.

Die! Die! Die in this love!
If you die in this love, Your soul will be renewed.
Die! Die! Don't fear the death of that which is known
If you die to the temporal, You will become timeless.

—Rumi

2. POTENTIAL

Potential is just that. It's the possibilities you contain within you. But nothing can happen in your life unless you do something, anything, to change it.

3. PEOPLE

It is your mindset and resolve, rather than your outward appearance, that goes a long way in determining all the important moments of your life.

4. PERSISTENCY

Persistency is the key to any success. The ability to stay the course, to put one foot in front of another, that is the secret.

5. PARAMETERS

Our lives up to this very second are basically an aggregation of a whole lot of experiences. They are your parameters. And the good news is that we can benefit from even those experiences that we would rather forget.

6. PUTTING FIRST

Helping others: it's a fundamental part of humanity, bonding together and helping a fellow man or woman. Some men and women even devote their lives to helping others, from the police force that protects our cities, to the fire departments whose members run into burning buildings, to the service men and women who risk their lives for the common good.

7. PROCESS

To keep yourself on task, you need to focus on the process of whatever is important to you. It will keep you involved instead of procrastinating or purposely not doing something.

8. PROGRESS

Here's what some of the greatest thinkers who have ever lived have in common; they didn't sit on their own hands and do nothing. If you know something, do something with that knowledge. And make it a habit; it will bring you ultimate power.

9. PRAYING

If you only say one prayer in a day make it "Thank You". - Rumi

If you would like more information regarding the 9 Ps, please contact me at yavuzaltun@happy.com.tr

Step Into Greatness

LES BROWN

You have greatness within you. You can do more than you could ever imagine. The problem most people have is that they set a goal and then ask "how can I do it? I don't have the necessary skills or education or experience".

I know what that's like. I wasted 14 years on asking myself how I could be a motivational speaker. My mind focused on the negative—on the things that were in my way, rather than on the things that were not.

It's not what you don't have but what you think you need that keeps you from getting what you want from life. But, when the dream is big enough, the obstacles don't matter. You'll get there if you stay the course. Nothing can stop you but death itself.

Think about that last statement for a minute. There's nothing on this earth that can stop you from achieving what it is that you want. So, get out of your way, and quit sabotaging your dreams. Do everything in your power to make them happen—because you cannot fail!

They say the best way to die is with your loved ones gathered around your bed. But what if you were dying and it was the ideas you never acted upon, the gifts you never used and the dreams you never pursued, that were circled around your bed? Answer that question right now. Write down your answers. If you die this very moment what ideas, what gifts, what dreams will die with you?

Then say: I refuse to die an unlived life! You beat out 40 million sperm to get here, and you'll never have to face such odds again. Walk through the field of life and leave a trail behind.

One day, one of my rich friends brought my mother a new pair of shoes for me. Now, even though we weren't well off, I didn't want them; they were a size nine and I was a size nine and a half. My mother didn't listen and told my sister to go get some Vaseline, which she rubbed all over my feet. Then my mother had me put those shoes on, minding that I didn't scrunch down the heel. She had my sister run some water in the bathtub, and I was told to get in and walk around in the water. I said that my feet hurt. She just ignored me and asked about my day at school, how everything went and did I get into any fights? I knew what she was up to, that she was trying to distract me, so I said I had only gotten into three fights. After a while mother asked me if my feet still hurt. I admitted that the pain had indeed lessened. She kept me walking in that tub until I had a brand new pair of comfortable, size nine and a half shoes.

You see, once the leather in the shoes got wet, they stretched! And what you need to do is stretch a little. I believe that most people don't set high goals and miss them, but rather, they set lower goals and hit them and then they stay there, stuck on the side of the highway of life. When you're pursuing your greatness, you don't know what your limitations are, and you need to act like you don't have any. If you shoot for the moon and miss, you'll still be in the stars.

You also need coaching (a mentor). Why? There are times you, too, will find yourself parked on the side of the highway of life with no gas in the vehicle. What you need then is someone to stop and offer to pick up some gas down the road a ways and bring it back to you. That person is your coach. Yes, they are there for advice, but their main job is to help you through the difficulties that life throws at all of us.

Another reason for having a coach is that you can't see the picture when you're in the frame. In other words, he or she can often see where you are with a clarity and focus that's unavailable to you. They're not going to leave you parked along the road of life, nor are they going to allow you to be stuck in the moment like a photo in a frame.

And let's say you just can't see you're way forward. You don't believe it's possible. Sometimes you just have to believe in someone's belief in you. This could be your coach, a loved one or even a staunch friend. You need to hear them say you can do it, time and again. Because, after all, faith comes from hearing and hearing and hearing.

Look at it this way. Most people fail because of possibility blindness. They can't see what lies before them. There are always possibilities. Because of this, your dream is possible. You may fail often. In fact, I want you to say this: I will fail my way to success. Here is why.

I had a TV show that failed. I felt I had to go back to public speaking. I had failed, so I parked my car for ten years. Then I saw Dr. Wayne Dyer was still on PBS and I decided to call them. They said they would love to work with me and asked where I had been. I wasn't as good as I had been ten years before, as I was out of practice, but I still had to get back in the game. I was determined to drive on empty.

Listen to recordings, go to seminars, challenge yourself, and you'll begin to step into your greatness, you'll begin to fill yourself with the energy you need to climb to ever greater heights. Most people never attend a seminar. They won't invest money in books or audio programs. You put yourself in the top 5 percent just by making a different choice than the average person. This is called contrary thinking. It's a concept taken from the financial industry. One considers choosing the exact opposite behaviour of the average person as a way to get better than average results. You don't have to make the contrarian choice, but if you don't have anything to lose by going that road, why not consider the option?

Make your move before you're ready. Walk by faith not by sight and make sure you're happy doing it. If you can't be happy, what else is there? Helen Keller said, "Life is short, eat the dessert first."

What is faith? Many of us think of God when we think of faith. A different viewpoint claims that faith is a firm belief in something for which there is no proof. I would rather think of faith as something that is believed especially with strong conviction. It is this last definition I am referring to when I say walk by faith not by sight. Be happy and go forth with strong conviction that you are destined for greatness.

An important step on your way to greatness is to take the time to detoxify. You've got to look at the people in your life. What are they doing for you? Are they setting a pace that you can follow? If not, whose pace have you adjusted to? If you're the smartest in your group, find a new group.

Are the people in your life pulling you down or lifting you up? You know what to do, right? Banish the negative and stay with the positive; it's that simple. Dr. Norman Vincent Peale once said (when I was in the audience), "You are special. You have greatness within you, and you can do more than you could ever possibly imagine."

He overrode the inner conversations in my mind and reached the heart of me. He set me on fire. This is yet another reason for seeking out the help of a coach or mentor or other new people in your life. They can do what Dr. Peale did for me. They can set your passion free.

How important is it to have the right kind of person/people on your side? There was a study done that determined it takes 16 people saying you can do something to overcome one person who says you can't do something. That's right, one negative, unsupportive person can wipe out the work of 16 other supportive people. The message can't be any clearer than that.

Let's face the cold, hard truth: most people stay in park along the highway of life. They never feel the passion, the love for their fellow man, or for the work they do. They are stuck in the proverbial rut. What's the reason? There are many reasons, but only one common factor: fear — fear of change, fear of failure, fear of success, fear they may not be good enough, fear of competition, even fear of rejection.

"Rejection is a myth," says Jack Canfield, co-author of The Chicken Soup for the Soul series. "It's not like you get a slap in the face each time you are rejected." Why not take every "no" you receive as a vitamin, and every time you take one know you are another step closer to success.

You will win if you don't quit. Even a broken clock is right twice a day.

Professional baseball players, on average, get on base just three times out of every ten times they face the opposing pitcher. Even superstars fail half of the time they appear at the plate.

Top commissioned salespeople face similar odds. They may make one sale from every three people they see, but it will have taken them between 75 and 100 telephone calls to make the 15 appointments they need to close their five sales for the week. And these are statistics for the elite. Most salespeople never reach these kinds of numbers.

People don't spend their lives working for just one company anymore. This means you must build up a set of skills and experiences that are portable. This can be done a number of ways, but my favourite approaches follow.

You must be willing to do the things others won't do in order to have tomorrow the things that others don't have. Provide more service than you get paid for. Set some high standards for yourself.

Begin each day with your most difficult task. The rest of the day will seem more enjoyable and a whole lot easier.

Someone needs help with a problem? Be the solution to that problem.

Also, find those tasks that are being consistently ignored and do them. You'll be surprised by the results. An acquaintance of mine used this approach at a number of entry-level positions and each time he quickly ended up being offered a position in management.

You must increase your energy. Kick it up a notch. We are spirits having a physical existence; let your spirit shine. Quit frittering away your energy. Use it to move you closer to the achievement of your dreams. Refuse to spend it on non-productive activities.

What do people say about you when you leave a room? Are you willing to take responsibility—to walk your talk. There is a terrible epidemic sweeping our nation, and it is the refusal to take responsibility for one's actions. Consider that at some point in any situation there will have been a moment where you could have done something to change the outcome. To that end you are responsible for what happened. It's a hard thing to accept, but it's true.

Life's hard. It was hard when I was told I had cancer. I had sunken into despair, and was hiding away in my study when my son came in. My son asked me if I was going to die. What could I do? I told him I was going to fight, even though I was scared. I also told him that I needed some help. Not because I was weak but because I wanted to stay strong. Keep asking until you get help. Don't stop until you get it.

A setback is the setup for a comeback. A setback is simply a misstep on the long road of success. It means nothing in the larger scheme of things. And, surprisingly, it sets you up for your next win. It tends to focus you and your energy on your immediate goals, paving the way for your next sprint, for your comeback.

It's worth it. Your dreams are worth the sacrifices you'll have to make to achieve them. Find five reasons that will make your dreams worth it for you. Say to yourself, I refuse to live an unlived life.

If you are casual about your dreams, you'll end up a casualty. You must be passionate about your dreams, living and breathing them throughout your days. You've got to be hungry! People who are hungry refuse to take no for an answer. Make NO your vitamin. Be unstoppable. Be hungry.

Let me give you an example of what I mean by hungry …

I decided I wanted to become a disc jockey, so I went down to the local

23

radio station and asked the manager, Mr. Milton "Butterball" Smith, if he had a job available for a disc jockey. He said he did not. The next day I went back, and Mr. Smith asked "Weren't you here yesterday?" I explained that I was just checking to see if anyone was sick or had died. He responded by telling me not to come back again. Day three, I went back again—with the same story. Mr. Smith told me to get out of there. I came back the fourth day and gave Mr. Smith my story one more time. He was so beside himself that he told me to get him a cup of coffee. I said, "Yes, sir!" That's how I became the errand boy.

While working as an errand boy at the station, I took every opportunity to hang out with the deejays and to observe them working. After I had taught myself how to run the control room, it was just a matter of biding my time.

Then one day an opportunity presented itself. One of the disc jockeys by the name of Rockin' Roger was drinking heavily while he was on the air. It was a Saturday afternoon. And there I was, the only one there.

I watched him through the control-room window. I walked back and forth in front of that window like a cat watching a mouse, saying "Drink, Rock, Drink!" I was young. I was ready. And I was hungry.

Pretty soon, the phone rang. It was the station manager. He said, "Les, this is Mr. Klein."

I said, "Yes, I know."

He said, "Rock can't finish his program."

I said, "Yes sir, I know."

He said, "Would you call one of the other disc jockeys to fill in?"

I said, "Yes sir, I sure will, sir."

And when he hung up, I said, "Now he must think I'm crazy." I called up my mama and my girlfriend, Cassandra, and I told them, "Ya'll go out on the front porch and turn up the radio, I'M ABOUT TO COME ON THE AIR!"

I waited 15 or 20 minutes and called the station manager back. I said, "Mr. Klein, I can't find NOBODY!"

He said, "Young boy, do you know how to work the controls?"

I said, "Yes, sir."

He said, "Go in there, but don't say anything. Hear me?"

I said, "Yes, sir."

I couldn't wait to get old Rock out of the way. I went in there, took my seat behind that turntable, flipped on the microphone and let 'er rip.

"Look out, this is me, LB., triple P. Les Brown your platter-playin' papa. There were none before me and there will be none after me, therefore that makes me the one and only. Young and single and love to mingle, certified, bona fide and indubitably qualified to bring you satisfaction and a whole lot of action. Look out baby, I'm your LOVE man."

I WAS HUNGRY!

During my adult life I've been a deejay, a radio station manager, a Democrat in the Ohio Legislature, a minister, a TV personality, an author and a public speaker, but I've always looked after what I valued most—my mother. What I want for her is one of my dreams, one of my goals.

My life has been a true testament to the power of positive thinking and the infinite human potential. I was born in an abandoned building on a floor in Liberty City, a low-income section of Miami, Florida, and adopted at six weeks of age by Mrs. Mamie Brown, a 38-year-old single woman, cafeteria cook and domestic worker. She had very little education or financial means, but a very big heart and the desire to care for myself and my twin brother. I call myself Mrs. Mamie Brown's Baby Boy and I say that all that I am and all that I ever hoped to be, I owe to my mother.

My determination and persistence in searching for ways to help my mother overcome poverty and developing my philosophy to do whatever it takes to achieve success led me to become a distinguished authority on harnessing human potential and success. That philosophy is best expressed by the following …

"If you want a thing bad enough to go out and fight for it,
to work day and night for it,
to give up your time, your peace and your sleep for it…
if all that you dream and scheme is about it,
and life seems useless and worthless without it…
if you gladly sweat for it and fret for it and plan for it
and lose all your terror of the opposition for it…
if you simply go after that thing you want
with all of your capacity, strength and sagacity,
faith, hope and confidence and stern pertinacity…
if neither cold, poverty, famine, nor gout,
sickness nor pain, of body and brain,
can keep you away from the thing that you want…
if dogged and grim you beseech and beset it,
with the help of God, you will get it!"

The 3 Things You Need to Become a Real Estate Millionaire

The Right Way to Invest Successfully

RAYMOND AARON

It seems like everywhere you look, someone is claiming that they became a millionaire by investing in real estate, and encouraging you to do the same. There are lots of TV shows about flipping houses for a fast buck that make it appear as if it's easy to find the right property and just as easy to sell it in a matter of months for a good profit. Unfortunately, that's not really how it works.

Investing in real estate is a proven way to make money, a lot of it. You could end up with millions, but you could also make a lot of very costly mistakes along the way. There has been so much hype about how easy it is to become a real estate millionaire that many people jump into the market without knowing what they are doing, and that's a shame, especially because qualified help is available.

Anyone can invest successfully in real estate if they have three things: a great real estate mentor, a proven real estate system, and a way to correctly predict the future. In other words, you need someone smart and knowledgeable to guide you, an understanding of the financial and legal aspects of buying, holding and selling real estate, and an ability to see societal trends and visualize how those trends will impact the real estate market.

A GREAT REAL ESTATE MENTOR

Investing on your own can be financially dangerous, especially for a first-timer. You're dealing with a lot of money, so any mistake can be a huge one. Buying at the wrong time in the cycle can kill your investments. And, regardless of the real estate strategy you employ, you're bound to hold onto properties for some period of time which means that severe negative cash flow and vacancies can ruin you. Plus, bad property management and a failure to know the most recent real estate and tax laws can get you sued.

An experienced mentor can help you choose the best real estate strategies for your situation, and the right properties in which to invest. They can also help you avoid the many possible pitfalls and make money while holding properties, and counsel you on when to sell for a great profit. Working with the right mentor can also keep real estate investing from becoming your full-time job.

Many people find that some part of the investment process is uncomfortable for them, whether it's initiating a conversation with a realtor, submitting an offer or hiring a property manager. A mentor can be very helpful in such situations as well.

In sum, learning from and working with the right mentor can make you a highly profitable investor in a relatively short period of time. Look for someone with years of experience and a proven track record.

A PROVEN SYSTEM

There's much more to investing in real estate than "buy low, sell high." To be successful, you must have the correct facts and the correct monthly habits concerning your real estate. Overall, you need to know what to buy, when to buy it, whether there will be a positive cash flow while you're holding on to it, and when to sell. Plus, what is the right low? What is the right high? How much money do you have to put down and how much income must be generated while you're waiting to sell?

Determining if a property is a good buy takes a lot of research and analysis. You will need to look at comparable purchase prices in the area, as well as rental fees. You'll also need to consider the location, the age and condition of the building, tax rates and about 30 other pieces of data. Evaluating the information for just one property could take you a day or more.

If you're serious about becoming a real estate investor, you are going to be considering quite a lot of properties on a regular basis. Even if you want to make investing your day job, you'll never have the time necessary to research fully and evaluate every property that comes to your attention. Hence, the first part of your system has to involve weeding out the lesser opportunities and focusing on the ones with potential.

The investors I mentor learn how to determine if a property is really a great deal in seconds. You only need two pieces of data: the purchase price and the current rent rate. Compare the two using a two-part formula. First, divide the asking price (outgoing funds) by 100. Then, given that current mortgage interest rates are below 8-10% divide the number you got by two. If the current monthly rent doesn't meet or better that second number, eliminate the property from consideration.

As an example, say the asking price is $1 million. If you divide it by 100, it comes out to $10 thousand. Divide again, by two, and you get $5 thousand. If the monthly rent isn't $5 thousand or more, you should pass on the property. You may miss out on a few winners using this system but, if you eliminate more properties than you think you should, you'll be successful and safe. Remember that, if interest rates rise significantly, you will need to adjust the formula to compensate.

Once you've weeded out the chaff from the wheat, do your due diligence on the remaining properties. Work closely with your mentor during this part of the process and, again, when it comes to making deals, say no more than you say yes. Just don't get cold feet or shy away from a great deal.

In terms of timing, it all comes down to momentum. There is always an overall upward momentum. Real estate prices go up and down, on an upwards track. So, one good profit strategy is to buy low, watch values rise and sell during the next boom. More precisely, you want to buy just as prices rise off the bottom (so that they're already rising) and sell when prices hit double the bottom, which is typically the very minimum prices rise to at the peak of the ensuing boom.

Don't attempt to predict the extremes — you will make a significant amount of money more safely buying just after prices begin rising (not the lowest point) and selling towards the end of the up period —without the risk associated with waiting too long and missing the highest point.

You'll also need a system for monitoring your investments while holding on until it's time to sell. Having a strong property manager is essential. So is reviewing rents taken in versus uncollectibles, repairs, and other expenses to ensure that your cash flow remains positive.

PREDICTING THE FUTURE

Good real estate investors learn to identify marketplace trends and buyers' or renters' needs. Start by investigating and tracking growth trends by neighborhood: are prices rising, is an area getting ready for a renaissance, are there new job opportunities nearby or is the area close to another neighborhood that's gotten too pricey?

Great real estate investors, however, go far beyond those basics. They look for large demographic or social elements that might provide the next big opportunity. The huge number of returning veterans after World War II led to a Baby Boom that provides the perfect example. Every stage of their lives brought an opportunity for marketers, real estate builders, and other manufacturers to fill unmet needs, be it starter homes for when they had children, tricycles for those children who were too young to ride a bike, or new sizes and types of cars. All of this was predictable, but no one noticed. Opportunities were capitalized upon as they arose, but imagine what financial success could have been attained if someone had predicted the Baby Boomers' needs in advance.

And, now, those Boomers are driving the growth of retirement communities and nursing homes. But, they are a more independent lot than their parents were, and have strived to remain young and healthy as long as possible. Quite a few of them can still live and thrive on their own, but many may need a little help at this point in their lives. They don't need or want an aide, nurse or social worker on a full-time basis and certainly aren't ready for a nursing home. That means there is a huge need for more up-to-date, internet-ready independent supportive living arrangements, of which there are too few. Investing in one now is bound to be a win.

Don't forget that those Baby Boomers had children of their own, and that created a mini baby boom. Think about the ways in which those children, now middle-aged adults, are different from their parents and what needs they might have, especially regarding real estate. You might also consider whether changes in the workforce, higher divorce rates and the economics of leaving home after college have implications for the real estate market as well. Keep your eyes and minds open!

Happiness: How to Experience the "Real Deals"

MARCI SHIMOFF

I was 41 years old, stretched out on a lounge chair by my pool and reflecting on my life. I had achieved all that I thought I needed to be happy.

You see, when I was a child, I thought there would be five main things that would ensure that I'd be happy: a successful career helping people, a loving husband, a comfortable home, a great body, and a wonderful circle of friends. After years of study, hard work, and a few "lucky breaks," I finally had them all. (Okay, so my body didn't quite look like Halle Berry's—but four out of five isn't bad!) You think I'd have been on the top of the world.

But surprisingly I wasn't. I felt an emptiness inside that the outer successes of life couldn't fill. I was also afraid that if I lost any of those things, I might be miserable. Sadly, I knew I wasn't alone in feeling this way.

While happiness is the one thing we all truly want, so few people really experience the deep and lasting fulfillment that fills our soul. Why aren't we finding it?

Because, in the words of the old country western song, we're looking for happiness in "all the wrong places."

Looking around, I saw that the happiest people I knew weren't the most successful and famous. Some were married, some were single. Some had lots of money, and some didn't have a dime. Some of them even had health challenges. From where I stood, there seemed to be no rhyme or reason to what made people happy. The obvious question became: *Could a person actually be happy for no reason?*

I had to find out.

So I threw myself into the study of happiness. I interviewed scores of scientists, as well as 100 unconditionally happy people. (I call them the Happy 100.) I delved into the research from the burgeoning field of positive psychology, the study of the positive traits that enable people to enjoy meaningful, fulfilling, and happy lives.

What I found changed my life. To share this knowledge with others, I wrote a book called *Happy for No Reason: 7 Steps to Being Happy from the Inside Out*.

One day, as I sat down to compile my findings, all the pieces of the puzzle fell into place. I had a simple, but profound "a-ha"—there's a continuum of happiness:

Unhappy: We all know what this means: life seems flat. Some of the signs are anxiety, fatigue, feeling blue or low—your "garden-variety" unhappiness. This isn't the same as clinical depression, which is characterized by deep despair and hopelessness that dramatically interferes with your ability to live a normal life, and for which professional help is absolutely necessary.

Happy for Bad Reason: When people are unhappy, they often try to make themselves feel better by indulging in addictions or behaviors that may feel good in the moment but are ultimately detrimental. They seek the highs that come from drugs, alcohol, excessive sex, "retail therapy," compulsive gambling, over-eating, and too much television-watching, to name a few. This kind of "happiness" is hardly happiness at all. It is only a temporary way to numb or escape our unhappiness through fleeting experiences of pleasure.

Happy for Good Reason: This is what people usually mean by happiness: having good relationships with our family and friends, success in our careers, financial security, a nice house or car, or using our talents and strengths well. It's the pleasure we derive from having the healthy things in our lives that we want.

Don't get me wrong. I'm all for this kind of happiness! It's just that it's only half the story. Being Happy for Good Reason depends on the external conditions of our lives—these conditions change or are lost, our happiness usually goes too. Relying solely on this type of happiness is where a lot of our fear is stemming from these days. We're afraid the things we think we need to be happy may be slipping from our grasp.

Deep inside, I think we all know that life isn't meant to be about getting by, numbing our pain, or having everything "under control." True happiness doesn't come from merely collecting an assortment of happy experiences. At our core, we know there's something more than this.

There is. It's the next level on the happiness continuum—Happy for No Reason.

Happy for No Reason: This is true happiness—a state of peace and well-being that isn't dependent on external circumstances.

Happy for No Reason isn't elation, euphoria, mood spikes, or peak experiences that don't last. It doesn't mean grinning like a fool 24/7 or experiencing a superficial high. Happy for No Reason isn't an emotion. In fact, when you are Happy for No Reason, you can have *any* emotion—including sadness, fear, anger or hurt—but you still experience that underlying state of peace and well-being.

When you're Happy for No Reason, you *bring* happiness to your outer experiences rather than trying to *extract* happiness from them. You don't need to manipulate the world around you to try to make yourself happy. You live from happiness, rather than *for* happiness.

This is a revolutionary concept. Most of us focus on being Happy for Good Reason, stringing together as many happy experiences as we can, like beads in a necklace, to create a happy life. We have to spend a lot of time and energy trying to find just the right beads so we can have a "happy necklace".

Being Happy for No Reason, in our necklace analogy, is like having a happy string. No matter what beads we put on our necklace—good, bad or indifferent—our inner experience, which is the string that runs through them all, is happy, and creates a happy life.

Happy for No Reason is a state that's been spoken of in virtually all spiritual and religious traditions throughout history. The concept is universal. In Buddhism, it is called causeless joy; in Christianity, the kingdom of Heaven within; and in Judaism it is called *ashrei*, an inner sense of holiness and health. In Islam it is called *falah*, happiness and well-being; and in Hinduism it is called *ananda*, or pure bliss. Some traditions refer to it as an enlightened or awakened state.

So how can you be Happy for No Reason?

Science is verifying the way. Researchers in the field of positive psychology have found that we each have a "happiness set-point," that determines our level of happiness. No matter what happens, whether it's something as exhilarating as winning the lottery or as challenging as a horrible accident, most people eventually return to their original happiness level. Like your weight set-point, which keeps the scale hovering around the same number, your happiness set-point will remain the same **unless you make a concerted effort to change it.** In the same way you'd crank up the thermostat to get comfortable on a chilly day, you actually have the power to reprogram your happiness set-point to a higher level of peace and well-being. The secret lies in practicing the habits of happiness.

Some books and programs will tell you that you can simply decide to be happy. They say just make up your mind to be happy—and you will be.

I don't agree.

You can't just decide to be happy, any more than you can decide to be fit or to be a great piano virtuoso and expect instant mastery. You can, however, decide to take the necessary steps, like exercising or taking piano lessons—and by practicing those skills, you can get in shape or give recitals. In the same way, you can become Happy for No Reason through practicing the habits of happy people.

All of your habitual thoughts and behaviors in the past have created specific neural pathways in the wiring in your brain, like grooves in a record. When we think or behave a certain way over and over, the neural pathway is strengthened and the groove becomes deeper—the way a well-traveled route through a field eventually becomes a clear-cut path. Unhappy people tend to have more negative neural pathways. This is why you can't just ignore the realities of your brain's wiring and *decide* to be happy! To raise your level of happiness, you have to create new grooves.

Scientists used to think that once a person reached adulthood, the brain was fairly well "set in stone" and there wasn't much you could do to change it. But new research is revealing exciting information about the brain's neuroplasticity: when you think, feel and act in different ways, the brain changes and actually rewires itself. You aren't doomed to the same negative neural pathways for your whole life. Leading brain researcher Dr. Richard Davidson, of the University of Wisconsin says, "Based on what we know of the plasticity of the brain, we can think of things like happiness and compassion as skills that are no different from learning to play a musical instrument or tennis …. it is possible to train our brains to be happy."

While a few of the Happy 100 I interviewed were born happy, most of them learned to be happy by practicing habits that supported their happiness. That means wherever you are on the happiness continuum, it's entirely in your power to raise your happiness level.

In the course of my research, I uncovered 21 core happiness habits that anyone can use to become happier and stay that way. You can find all 21 happiness habits at www.HappyForNoReason.com

Here are a few tips to get you started:

1. **Incline Your Mind Toward Joy.** Have you noticed that your mind tends to register the negative events in your life more than the positive? If you get ten compliments in a day and one criticism, what do you remember? For most people, it's the criticism. Scientists call this our "negativity bias" — our primitive survival wiring that causes us to pay more attention to the negative than the positive. To reverse this bias, get into the daily habit of consciously registering the positive around you: the sun on your skin, the taste of a favorite food, a smile or kind word from a co-worker or friend. Once you notice something positive, take a moment to savor it deeply and feel it; make it more than just a mental observation. Spend 20 seconds soaking up the happiness you feel.

2. **Let Love Lead.** One way to power up your heart's flow is by sending loving kindness to your friends and family, as well as strangers you pass on the street. Next time you're waiting for the elevator at work, stuck in a line at the store or caught up in traffic, send a silent wish to the people you see for their happiness, well-being, and health. Simply wishing others well switches on the "pump" in your own heart that generates love and creates a strong current of happiness.

3. **Lighten Your Load.** To make a habit of letting go of worries and negative thoughts, start by letting go on the physical level. Cultural anthropologist Angeles Arrien recommends giving or throwing away 27 items a day for nine days. This deceptively simple practice will help you break attachments that no longer serve you.

4. **Make Your Cells Happy.** Your brain contains a veritable pharmacopeia of natural happiness-enhancing neurochemicals — endorphins, serotonin, oxytocin, and dopamine — just waiting to be released to every organ and cell in your body. The way that you eat, move, rest, and even your facial expression can shift the balance of your body's feel-good-chemicals, or "Joy Juice", in your favor. To dispense some extra Joy Juice — smile. Scientists have discovered that smiling decreases stress hormones and boosts happiness chemicals, which increase the body's T-cells, reduce pain, and enhance relaxation. You may not feel like it, but smiling — even artificially to begin with — starts the ball rolling and will turn into a real smile in short order.

5. **Hang with the Happy.** We catch the emotions of those around us just like we catch their colds — it's called emotional contagion. So it's important to make wise choices about the company you keep. Create appropriate boundaries with emotional bullies and "happiness vampires" who suck the life out of you. Develop your happiness "dream team" — a mastermind or support group you meet with regularly to keep you steady on the path of raising your happiness.

"Happily ever after" isn't just for fairytales or for only the lucky few. Imagine experiencing inner peace and well-being as the backdrop for everything else in your life. When you're Happy for No Reason, it's not that your life always looks perfect — it's that, however it looks, you'll still be happy!

By Marci Shimoff. Based on the New York Times bestseller *Happy for No Reason: 7 Steps to Being Happy from the Inside Out*, which offers a revolutionary approach to experiencing deep and lasting happiness. The woman's face of the *Chicken Soup for the Soul* series and a featured teacher in *The Secret*, Marci is an authority on success, happiness, and the law of attraction. To order *Happy for No Reason* and receive free bonus gifts, go to www.happyfornoreason.com/mybook.

Go Ahead, Give Yourself Permission to Dream Big

BRIARLEY NICHOLSON

I saw my home go up in flames on Christmas Day, when I was barely seven. Our farm was invaded during the civil war in Zimbabwe (then Rhodesia), petrol poured over and around the house, a struck match thrown in. We escaped death because, fortunately, we were in the city of Harare with our grandmother on Christmas Eve, when the invasion occurred.

I escaped an attempted rape at school, when I was 11.

I grew up in a country where, at its worst, hyperinflation was officially 13.2 billion % per month. This meant that money had to be spent the moment it was earned because, come tomorrow, it wouldn't be worth the paper it was printed on. The good part was I became a trillionaire very quickly, and I still hold a $100,000,000,000,000 note (and 13 zero's have been removed!)

However, here I am. I wasn't born with a silver spoon in my mouth. Despite a currency whose value slipped like sand through the fingertips, and on occasion not having two cents to rub together, I've done the things I've set out to do, overcome the challenges, and become the person I sought to be. I love what I do, helping people transform to greater success, achieve financial freedom and live life with passion on their own terms.

I'm not anyone especially gifted. I wasn't an A student nor did I seek academic honours. I did, however, desire to travel and, by going for my dreams, I transitioned through South Africa as the first step, and then moved to London. I worked hard, saved, kept out of debt and travelled around the world, realizing my passion for global adventures.

I discovered that going for my dreams was easier than I ever thought possible, and it was a whole lot of fun.

I've made big leaps in personal transformation by studying first-hand with some of the world's greatest coaches including Tony Robbins, Robert Kiyosaki, Matt Morris, Marc Accetta, Johnny Wimbrey, Scott Harris, Harv T Eker, Les Brown, Raymond Aaron, to name a few.

Along the way, I created a simple-to-follow system for financial empowerment that kept yielding consistent and repeatable successes. By adhering to tried and true strategies, I made huge quantum leaps in my life. My life is richer and fuller because I was willing to reach out for what life had to offer and take a chance.

Pretty good for a young farm girl from a small mining town, Bindura, in Zimbabwe.

Each of us has untold potential within us, and it's there for the taking, no matter the cards we've been dealt.

Do any of these sound familiar?

- Weighed down by too much debt?

- Trapped in an undesirable job?

- Can't stop the spending habit?

- Working too hard for too little?

- Held back by fear and insecurities?

- Feeling something's missing?

- Finding instant gratification doesn't work?

- Afraid of the future?

- Feeling you're owed it, why should you work for it?

- Never got time?

Do you want the next chapters of your life to be more of the same or do you want to live the life you've always dreamt of? If you say "yes" to a dream life with more ease, more fun, more success, read on.

TIME TESTED, EASY, MANAGEABLE PRINCIPLES

I'm going to share some of my success principles with you to create the financial freedom and independence you deserve. These are the same strategies that I use in my coaching consultations, my online seminars and my workshops.

1. Now is All You Have, Don't Waste it

The time that you have is your most precious commodity. Once it's come and gone, it stays gone. You can't rewind that clock nor reclaim the days, months and years you've lost. You can lose money and make more, but you can NEVER make more time.

What this means is that you act now. You take action now; even if they are small steps, you take them consistently, at full tilt.

There's no perfect moment when everything falls into place.

Maybe you are dithering and spinning "what ifs" in your head because you are afraid of making mistakes.

It's quite simple, really. If you do nothing while waiting for the perfect moment, nothing is what you get back. There is no perfect moment. Life is life.

2. Give Yourself Permission to Dream Big

Dream big, and then dream even bigger. It's your life, if you don't dare to dream the things you want, who's going to do it for you? Your family, your friends, your partner? No, they've their own lives to lead.

Maybe right now you're saying, "Briarley, that's just silly daydreaming. I dream of becoming a millionaire, but look at where I am. No way am I becoming a millionaire unless I buy a winning ticket."

Let me tell you otherwise.

Matt Morris, celebrated author and one of my mentors, was at 21 years homeless, $30,000 in the red, and lived out of the back of his car. By the time he turned 24, he was earning six-figures, and by 29 he had made his millions.

He gave himself permission to dream of being a millionaire. Starved and hungry in the back of his car, wishing for millions in his bank account was not very sensible or doable, was it? But he didn't doubt himself. Instead, he went after his dream, without looking back.

Don't edit yourself; instead raise the bar on your dreams.

Remember nothing happens without you first thinking or dreaming about it.

"If you can imagine it, you can achieve it. If you can dream it, you can become it"

"Winners Never Quit and Quitters Never Win"

These are my favorite quotes on success, and ones that I live by. You never give up on your dream. It may take longer than you expected, there may be a few more bumps on the road, but it is always possible. A great book that illustrates this most is "The Impossible Just Takes a Little Longer" by Art Berg. I always dreamed of having children and a family; life turned out differently, probably because of my independence, and when I started trying for kids I could not conceive. I was so determined at never quitting that, despite doctors telling me I had no eggs left and would have to get an egg donor, my mindset was right and I conceived naturally. Today I have the most amazing son, Ricky. DREAM and NEVER QUIT!!!

3. Fear is Just a Four-Letter Word

There is a space for such four letter words – the junk pile. Fear becomes bigger than it really is when we feed it, and it grows fat on our anxieties and concerns.

Some of you may fear failure. You worry that you'll become the laughing stock of your circle and lose any esteem in the eyes of others. You must have a strong reason WHY you want to achieve, to ignore the bystanders (because that is what they are).

But look at the success stories of today, pick any models of success, read up on their life stories and you'll see that what differentiated them was that they didn't let their fears hold them back. They stared fear in the face and, guess who flinched first? Not them. 99% of what one worries about never actually happens anyway.

Even if they made mistakes, and big ones too, these successful men and women took notes from their experiences and applied those lessons to becoming even more successful in the future.

When we see fear for really what it is – just a four letter word – we can hurdle over it and run forward with ease towards what we want.

4. Keep Your Eye on the Prize

I'm not going to lie and tell you it's easy. You may have to work harder than you've ever had to.

I held two jobs in South Africa for eighteen months to earn enough to buy my first airline ticket to London. Once there, I shared a house with 13 others, held three jobs -- a full-time secretarial job, weekend days as a sales representative, and weekend nights serving behind a bar. I worked hard, went without and made sacrifices.

By regularly depositing my salary into a savings account and living off my weekend earnings, I realized my dream of visiting exotic countries and immersing myself in colorful cultures.

Did I find it hard going? Sometimes, but I kept my eye on the prize – being a global traveler – and I kept going and had a blast doing so.

Later, trying to fall pregnant, I was faced with turbulent emotions, hormone imbalances, drugs and financial challenges. I observed unwanted pregnancies in other people, noticed neglected children, encountered the fear of never having a child, and the list goes on. It was not easy at all; however, I had my eye on the prize and only the prize. There was no room for doubt. I won!

That's because I realized that everything I did got me closer to my dreams.

5. MAP – A Small Word That Packs a Mighty Punch

MAP stands for two things.

Firstly, it stands for map, the guidance system that you need to get you from here to there.

If you were driving a car, you'll turn on your GPS system, figure how long it will take, get fuel to make sure you are not stranded, and turn on the music (in my case, it is Personal Development). If it's a long journey, you may look for place to refuel and renew. You'll find the data you need to guide you along the pathway with a map.

MAP also stands for Massive Action Plan, and it starts with being very clear with your goals. By knowing what you want to achieve and why, you identify the true purpose behind a goal.

Once you understand true purpose, you'll be able to connect the dots between desire, action and results.

You'll be able to monitor whether you are taking the right steps that are producing the right outcomes, or whether you are being side-tracked by detours or non-essential action.

You get three powerful benefits out of a MAP.

I. It provides clarity.

Many people quit because they lose their sense of direction. They get bored. And they end up where they don't want to be.

A MAP allows you to correct course. If you feel you're pursuing the wrong goal, you know to go back to basics.

Understand the purpose why you are reaching for a specific goal. As you probe beneath the surface, you may realize you have set this goal because it's expected of you. Not because you really want it for yourself.

Time to reset and get back on track.

II. It strengthens commitment.

You get to pat yourself on the back and celebrate when you get results that you desire. Knowing that you're doing absolutely the right things towards your goals is a pretty big motivator. It lifts you up and fills you with positive, boundless energy. When you're so filled with such excitement and energy, you're unstoppable.

That's massive action.

III. It empowers.

MAP is result-orientated. By breaking what you need to do into small, specific steps, you kick-start yourself into making moves and, before you know it, you're that much closer to your goals because of the momentum you've created.

More importantly, you're self-directing the action towards your goals to realize your desires.

You're taking back control, rather than being controlled by external circumstances. That's real power.

These are some of the dynamic strategies available to you to turn your life around, wire into the potential that lies within and create greater fulfillment.

HERE'S EVEN MORE GOOD NEWS

An exciting journey lies ahead of you, to move from financial distress to financial empowerment, from a ho-hum life to a life of greatness. Here are a few more lessons I learned along the way, on my own path to discovery.

• Passion turns hard work into fun

All of us have experienced this. We don't notice time passing, we are not bothered by distractions and we even forget when we are hungry when we are fully engaged in something that fires up our passion.

Passion taps into your own personal power and strengths, some of which may be hidden. It is your fuel when the going gets bumpy and it is your best weapon to make your dreams come true.

Look within to find out what fires you up.

• Commit, follow through, be accountable

Commitment follows from purpose. It's easy to stay gung-ho when the going is easy but what happens when it becomes challenging?

Stay focused. Remind yourself it is your life, remember your purpose, keep walking forward, remain curious. Life rewards you greatly when you dare. Think abundance not scarcity.

Turn up when you say you will, deliver what you promise to do, and be responsible for your successes and your mistakes.

By always following through and staying accountable, you are shaping within yourself a priceless habit of consistency. When you do it often enough, like any habit, it becomes second nature and it stays with you for life.

• You don't have to walk alone

A journey of a thousand steps may seem like a very lonely path. Here's the good news. You don't have to do it alone.

There are workshops, mastery seminars, masterminded groups, online forums, like-minded travelers, mentors, coaches. There are boundless resources and opportunities.

Reaching out for your dreams sounds like a big lofty idea. However, I support you with easy, practical and manageable how-to-tips in my book, online courses and coaching consultations that can be applied immediately. You get simple, solid steps for how to take action now; not next week or next month, but right now.

They are time-tested how-to tips and proven strategies. As you achieve successes in small steps, you can add more and more as you feel comfortable to build up momentum towards financial empowerment, freedom and a purposeful, fulfilling life.

The next step is yours to take.

A successful life and financial transformational coach, Briarley Nicholson is an entrepreneur and has her own successful businesses in financial advisory, money management, management accounting, network marketing, coaching and property investing, and loves to travel and meet people. Briarley is passionate about using her professional training and life experiences to make a difference in people's lives. She helps her clients develop breakthrough strategies to achieve financial freedom and design a life of their dreams.

Email: briarleynicholson@gmail.com
Facebook: @CoachBriarley
Tel: +1 727 214 5977

Motivation Does Activate and Sustain Behaviour

How to Bring Results in Life and Business

JULIE HOGBIN

B efore we talk about motivation in any great detail, it would be a good idea to cover the basics about what motivation really is. There are many, many, theories and huge amounts of research has been conducted on the subject over many decades. To be honest, with all the information out there it can be confusing as to what it all means.

One thing is for sure, one theory — one piece of information — does not cover it all as each researcher has their own bent and interpretation on the subject. It is when you are able to link it all together that it starts to make sense and you are able to do something with the information to help yourself.

I have researched, read about, practiced, and taught this subject to over 20,000 Leaders in Life, Business and the Entrepreneur market, both one-on-one and in small groups for very nearly three decades, and I am still learning.

This chapter is based around my knowledge, my interpretation, and a definition of Motivation that I have worked with for a long time. I have neither found nor developed a better definition — yet!

"Motivation is a conscious or unconscious driving force that arouses and directs action towards the achievement of a desired goal."

ClaimYourDestiny.global   #ConsciousLeadership

So, what does this mean in reality? It means that we are motivated by internal and external factors and that sometimes we know what those factors are and sometimes we don't: Our actions and thoughts are both conscious and unconscious in nature. It also means that the motives provoke a reaction and an action that help us 'get' something we want — a goal — and as a driving force they are powerful.

So my 1st questions to you are:

• What is your goal?

• What are you working towards?

• How many goals do you have?

- What is driving you?

- How conscious are you?

Motivation is an internal force; we are the only ones who can motivate us. Motivation can be affected by external influences. Ultimately it is us, and only us, that make the decision to do or not to do something. Nobody can make you feel or do anything! It is your absolute choice to capitulate and do, or to resist and not do.

We make the decision based on the information we have at the time and how confident we feel. There are many emotions and personal characteristics that come into play when we are talking about motivation and all that entails.

When we say that others motivate us what it really means is that they have created an environment that inspires us to do something. We make the decision out of fear in some cases, because we know it makes sense in other cases, because we aspire to be like the individual, or, more simply, just because we want to.

For you, and everybody else, your desired goal always provides you with a positive outcome. It gives you something you want even if that want is unconsciously driven. For others viewing it from their perspective, that outcome may be viewed as negative.

Let me explain what I mean with a couple of examples.

Addicts of any description do whatever it takes to fuel their need. They are achieving their desired outcome with more alcohol, more food, less food, more drugs, or just more of something, and they will go to extreme lengths to get it, such as selling personal and other people's belongings, lying and deceiving, going into debt and stealing.

Someone comes home with great intent of doing some research, maybe to write a book or to do some personal development such as going to the gym, and they end up sitting in front of the TV for hours with a bottle of wine. What is their driving force? We may not understand it as the viewer but there is definitely one for the person being observed.

Let's look at a couple of positive examples with a more generally accepted encouraging outcome.

A young person decides what they want to achieve in their life. They study like crazy to get the grades required to get to the top university and to study in a class of four with the top professor in their subject matter field, and they achieve it.

An individual from an underprivileged background wants to change their life, achieve greater things than have ever been achieved in their family, and become independently wealthy, and they are successful in achieving their goals.

Now for every example shared the opposite can be true as well. Not everybody becomes an addict, not everyone slouches in front of the TV, not every student achieves their potential, and not every underprivileged individual becomes independently wealthy.

"Everything you do is goal-driven. Everything you do is because you want the end result — whatever that end result may be!"

ClaimYourDestiny.global   #ConsciousLeadership

The examples are all based on how motivated the individual is to achieve their goal. Now if you know your goal consciously, can keep it in focus and resist the temptation of your old ways, you can achieve marvellous results.

The rest of this chapter will look at what drives you and how you can change your habits and behaviours over a period both short and long term, with the aim to achieve whatever it is you want.

I reference no theory in this chapter. There are many to read and learn which are of use to us all intellectually and unless the theory is practically applied and interpreted into reality all they remain are theories. I have spent decades interpreting theories into real life behaviours that make a difference for the better.

A few more questions for you to think about first.

- What are your drivers?

- What are your values?

- What is your risk tolerance?

- How much do you want to fit in with the 'norm' of your social group?

- How much do you really want, on a scale of 1 to 10, the thing it is you are aiming to achieve?

- How comfortable are you with change?

There are a lot more questions to ask but these will start you on the journey to understand your own motivators.

"Your motives create your habits, for good and bad, as they are your driving force."

ClaimYourDestiny.global   #ConsciousLeadership

There is so much information coming at us on a minute by minute basis. We make thousands upon thousands of decisions every day — so many in fact, we cannot be conscious of all the decisions, to do or not to do something, that we do make. We would be completely overwhelmed if we did.

So what do we do? We create patterns of behaviour that we do not have to think about, as it is quicker that way, to achieve our outcomes. We create habits that get us what we want in the easiest manner.

"Your habits have created your behaviour through your values, beliefs, and attitudes."

ClaimYourDestiny.global   #ConsciousLeadership

HABITS

Habits are a set of thoughts, behaviours, and ways of being that are developed through repeated behaviour. Habits are formed from the moment we become aware that there is a 'norm' of how to do things. Some we pick up from our parents, guardians, siblings, and influential individuals around us at a very early age. Others we develop for ourselves through the maturing process.

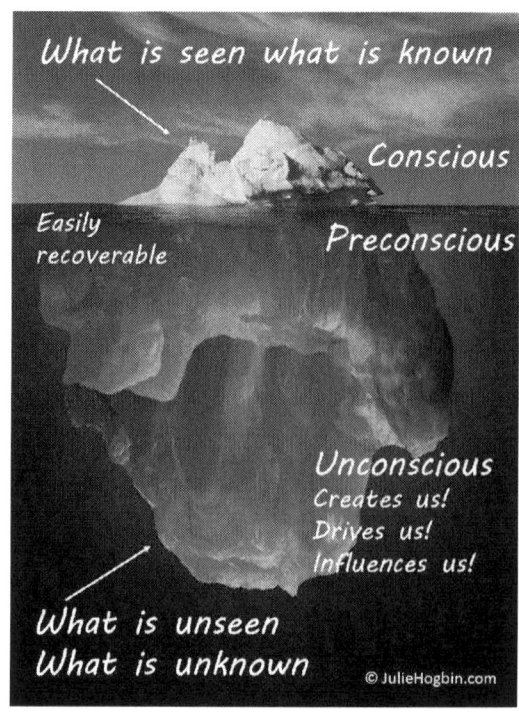

"Look to your parents for your beliefs about the world and yourself – you may be amazed at the similarities."

ClaimYourDestiny.global   #ConsciousLeadership

Once habits are created they can be difficult to break. To break a habit, we must consciously think about doing something different and then do it — which can equal hard work and being uncomfortable.

The thing is, we can all break habits if we really want to. BUT (and there is a big BUT) the unconscious part of our being is there to keep us safe. Any change and it may feel we are under threat and revert quickly to the old ways.

"Talk to your unconscious and ask its permission if you want to change some deep held habits and motivations to do things in a new way."

"Sounds a bit weird? Well it works, try it for yourself."

ClaimYourDestiny.global   #ConsciousLeadership

VALUES

Your values are a central part of who you are and who you want to be. By becoming more aware of these driving motivators in your life, you can use them as a guide to make the best choice in any situation.

Your decisions and actions, when in line with your values, will be easy to make and put into practice. If you are attempting to do something that is not held as a value to you, you will find it harder to do and, potentially, you will be in conflict with yourself.

Here is an example. If one of your values is honesty and you are in a relationship, business or personal, with someone who you know tells untruths, how hard will you find it to trust them? What will this do to your behaviour and your motivation within the relationship?

Values can be worked with, reordered, and installed — so do not lose hope. I personally have needed to work hard on my value regarding money. To say the least, it was slightly askew!

ATTITUDES

Your attitude is a predisposition to respond either negatively or positively towards an idea, object, person, or situation. It is the way you feel about something or someone. It can also be a particular feeling or opinion. It is seen as a conscious behaviour but will come from an unconscious driver.

Your attitude evolves as a result of your beliefs and values and will influence:

- Your choice of action and behaviour

- Your response to challenges

- Your response to incentives

- Your response to a word

- Your response to someone trying to help you

We all have an attitude — we cannot not have one. Generally, when it is said someone has an attitude it is meant as a negative opinion, but attitudes are drivers for good as well. It is just a common adaptation of a word which is more often linked to negativity.

As with anything else we do, our attitude is a choice we make. My choice, and I trust yours as you are reading this book, is to start each day with a positive attitude — it soon becomes a habit.

If you want to change something in your life, surround yourself with those who are on the same path or learn from those who have already done the 'thing' that you want to do. Attitudes are contagious so eradicate those personally held by yourself and those that are owned by people that may be in your circle who aren't helping you. If you don't know what your attitudes are, ask someone for feedback who will tell you the truth.

Also carefully study your close associates to make your own decisions on who stays with you on your journey and who leaves, their attitudes can be contagious. Look at the relationships that are in your life and acknowledge whether they are supporting you or hindering you. Decisions then can be made from a realistic position of what you want to do.

SOCIAL INTELLIGENCE

Social intelligence indicates that portions of our knowledge acquisition can be directly related to observing others within the context of social interactions, experiences and media influences.

So what does this mean to all of us? Basically, it means that if we see something that is rewarded, we copy it so that we get rewarded. We achieve the same result as we have observed, therefore we have achieved our result, which was our goal. There is far more to it but that's the basic concept. We learn by example from others.

So who do we copy? We copy those close to us and we adopt behaviours to fit into the crowd and belong. As we get older, we copy those who we admire or those who we aspire to be like. We develop a sense of self and become more aware of what it is we want. We begin to lead rather than follow — well some of us do and I expect you are a leader since you are reading this book! Join my Facebook group for more, https://www.facebook.com/groups/ClaimYourDestiny/

We are motivated to belong to a group with a certain set of characteristics. That could be because it is what we want or it can be because we know no different. It can be through peer pressure or choice, but whichever route we take it is ultimately our choice!

Join my Facebook group for more, https://www.facebook.com/groups/ClaimYourDestiny/

It is these drivers of behaviour that make you act differently from, or the same as, others in any given situation. So, by understanding these drivers, you

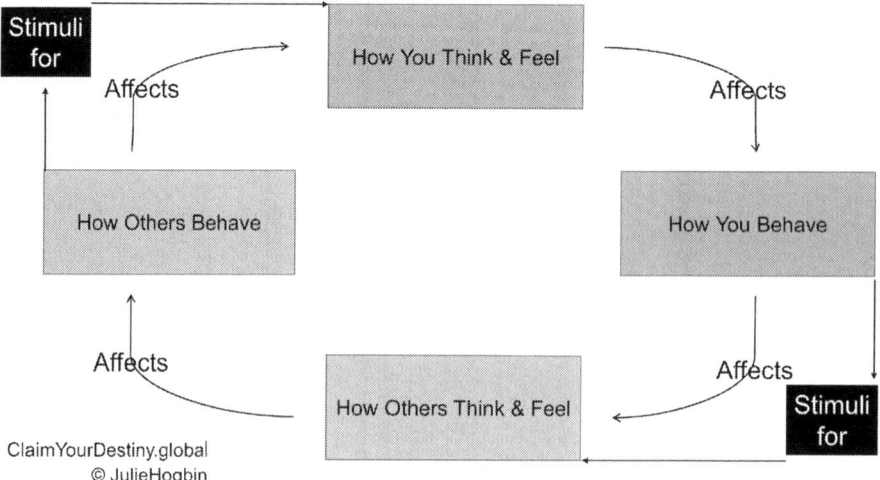

can better understand why you do the things you do. The skill is not only to understand your conscious needs, but also those that are unconscious in nature.

"In the choice between changing one's mind and proving there's no need to do so, most people get busy on the proof."

-John Kenneth Galbraith

SELF-PERCEPTION

Self-perception is the belief or disbelief in our own capabilities to achieve a goal or an outcome. These beliefs provide the foundation for human motivation, well-being, and personal accomplishment. This is because unless you believe that your actions can produce the outcomes you desire, you will have little incentive to act or to persevere in the face of difficulties.

Of course, human functioning is influenced by many factors. The success or failure you experience as you engage the countless tasks that comprise your life naturally influences the many decisions you must make. Also, the knowledge and skills you possess will certainly play critical roles in what you choose to do and not do.

"People's level of motivation, emotional states, and actions are based more on what they believe than on what is objectively true. For this reason, how you behave can often be better predicted by the beliefs you hold about your capabilities than by what you are actually capable of accomplishing."

ClaimYourDestiny.global   #ConsciousLeadership

You only need to watch one of the reality TV shows to see how clearly some people are deluded about their own abilities. The opposite is also true — you talk to someone who you know is gifted and they think and believe the complete opposite.

Our upbringing and early influencers, or even a recent happening, have a huge part to play in how and what we believe about ourselves. The great news though is whatever has happened in the past does not have to happen in our future.

These perceptions help determine what you do with the knowledge and skills you have. They also explain why your behaviours are sometimes not matched to your actual capabilities and why your behaviour may differ widely from somebody else, even when you have similar knowledge and skills.

For example, many talented people suffer frequent (and sometimes debilitating) bouts of self-doubt about capabilities they clearly possess, just as many individuals are confident about what they can accomplish despite possessing a modest repertoire of skills. Belief and reality are seldom perfectly matched, and individuals are typically guided by their beliefs when they engage the world.

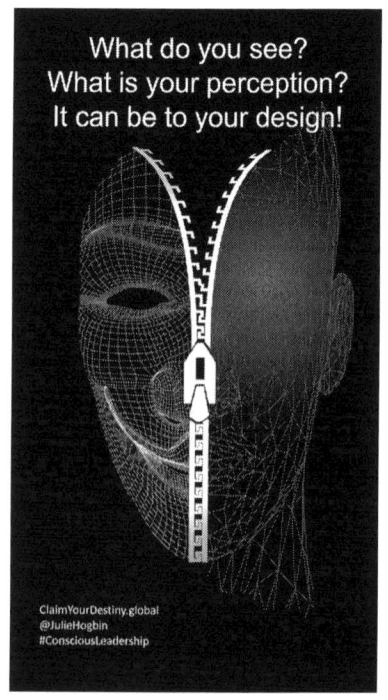

What do you see?
What is your perception?
It can be to your design!

ClaimYourDestiny.global
@JulieHogbin
#ConsciousLeadership

As a consequence, your accomplishments are generally better predicted by your self-perception than by your previous achievements, knowledge, or skills. Of course, no amount of confidence or self-appreciation can produce success when requisite skills and knowledge are absent.

"Skills and knowledge can all be gained if you want them enough and you find the right mentor to teach you."

ClaimYourDestiny.global   #ConsciousLeadership

COLLECTIVE PERCEPTION

Because individuals operate collectively as well as individually, self-perception is both a personal and a social construct. Collective systems develop a sense of collective effectiveness, it can create the group's shared belief in its capability to attain goals and accomplish desired tasks.

One brain is one but the collective brainpower of a group equals more than the sum of its parts — it's the adage $1+1=3$ or $2+2=5$. However, this is only true when the collective works together in harmony with the same aim. If members of the collective are working against each other one brain doesn't even equate to one — it will function at a lesser capability, as will the individual as they will be experiencing conflict.

For example, organisations develop collective beliefs about the capability of their salesforce to perform, of their managers to teach and otherwise enhance the lives of their workforce, and of their administrators and policymakers to create environments conducive to these tasks. Organisations, as well as individuals, also create beliefs that are not positive — they cannot gain additional sales, clients, revenue, etc. Collectiveness creates a culture which needs to be managed.

Organisations with a strong sense of positive collective perception exercise empowering and vitalising influences over their employees. These effects are evident in their results.

The power of others' attitudes (as mentioned previously) are contagious and will affect your motivation. If you are in the company of a high sender of negative emotion, you will be affected. If you are in the company of a high sender of positivity, it will be less influential.

As the saying goes, it only takes one bad apple to spoil the barrel.

Weed out the bad apples and your motivation will improve. Take on more of the good apples that are doing the same thing that you want to do and your motivation will improve by leaps and bounds.

CHOICES

Only you can justify the choices you make and most of you will make your choices in reference to past experiences rather than future opportunities. Change how you think and you will change your future.

"The definition of insanity is doing the same thing over and over again and expecting a different result."

– Albert Einstein

How do you change to get a different result? It's easy, think differently and take different actions. Open your mind and your being to possibilities; your past does not have to equal your future. With #ConsciousLeadership it can all change.

Every thought, every action, and every decision you make takes you closer to, or further away, from where you want to be. The smallest of decisions compounded over time creates massive change. Rather than attempt to make a huge change overnight, which can be scary and overwhelming, make small incremental changes that lead you towards your goal.

What do I mean? 5 minutes exercise a day wont make much difference if you do or don't do it BUT 5 minutes everyday will. A cake on one day wont make much difference to your health BUT a cake every day will (in the wrong direction). Delaying cutting the lawn for one day wont make much difference BUT delaying every day will.

Even doing nothing takes you further away because everything else is moving forward. The skills of yesteryear will not suffice in the next year. Think about how technology changes. If you haven't kept up with the last change you will soon be a very long way behind!

Sometimes, it can be a life-changing event that allows you to make the decision to do something immediately that you have tried before and failed at. A friend of mine, when diagnosed with cancer, stopped smoking overnight after 40 years. Please do not leave it until that type of thing happens before you change. Take on board #ConsciousLeadership now and change your life for the better, it is your choice!

Start to work now on different decisions for what you want and need:

- Why wait to be taken through a disciplinary process at work before you improve your skills or performance?

- Why wait until you are so over or underweight before you change your nutrition intake?

- Why wait until you cannot walk upstairs without puffing before you increase your fitness level?

- Why wait until you are close to retirement to think about how much money you need to live on and enjoy your retirement?

Through reading, applying, and practicing the experiences of others, you can learn what has worked for those before you, and you can apply those principles in your own life.

Motivational states are directive, they guide behaviours toward satisfying specific goals or specific needs. Do you have clearly defined goals? If you don't, sit down now, identify what it is you really want or need, and write that down. Then create a plan of how you will achieve it. This will provide you with motivation to do things differently.

If you want more information on how to this, I can highly recommend my book 'The Life Changing Magic of Setting Goals'. It is available from Amazon or through ClaimYourDestiny.global

"Change begins with your awareness that your beliefs are a choice; all beliefs, conscious or unconscious, are based on a choice."

ClaimYourDestiny.global   #ConsciousLeadership

There are a myriad of choices to be made all of the time. If you choose a different way to do something, gather information that allows you to make an educated choice for action. Do your research and due diligence and pick the best solution for you.

This will enhance your confidence, create new knowledge, quieten the inner doubting voice, match your values, enhance your beliefs, or question them to bolster your attitude.

This will allow you to convince your unconscious that you are looking after it and it will help you. Provide your unconscious with the reason why you are making alternate choices to that of the past and it will support you all the way.

DELAYED GRATIFICATION

There have been many studies done related to the benefits of delayed gratification. What does this really mean? It means living with the future in mind rather than the present.

In this world of instant gratification, keeping up with the Joneses, wearing the right designer labels, being influenced by adverts that say you must have this face cream and that aftershave, feeling like your holidays must become bigger and more expensive, having to change your car every two years, etc. It can be hard to resist the instant temptation, to be outside the norm, or to exclude yourself from your friends' activities.

In the moment, sometimes it can seem obvious to take the reward, and worry about the future in the future.

Your choice is dependent on your goals, your drivers, your beliefs (and how strong they are), and how strong your will to resist temptation is.

If you can recognise when you have an opportunity for a larger or more important reward, it shows you know the difference between your needs and your wants. When you can recognise these situations, there are key terms you must think of.

Patience, will, and self-control are all characteristics of people who are masters of their environment. One common challenge is postponing immediate gratification in the pursuit of long-term goals. Delayed gratification is the process of transcending immediate temptations to achieve long-term goals.

Knowing how to create, manage, and control your goals is the first step towards completing the things you want most in life; with a goal, we engage our brain to work toward it.

Think of goals as roadmaps designed to keep you on target. They make the experience and the journey possible and more enjoyable. They, in fact, become priorities that drive our actions. They become motivators.

Let me ask you once again:

- What are your long-term goals?
  And for some of you

- What are your short-term goals?

If you do not have goals sit down now and plan them for yourself, tell yourself and others they are important, write them down and believe you are worthy of them and you will achieve them. Focus on them and they will become a reality

See
Say
Write
Believe
Achieve

THE POWER OF QUESTIONS

Questions, when constructed in the right way, are the most powerful way

to access your beliefs. And this works irrespective of who asks the question. Ask yourself a question and your mind will do its best to provide you with an answer. The better your question, the better the answer.

Do you want to spend the rest of your life figuring out how to get the things you desire, or would you rather put all the guesswork behind you and get down to the fun of building an out-of-this-world lifestyle? Easy choice, right? Then do yourself a favour: suspend your disbelief, lower your shields, and try a simple way of improving your life.

Identify someone you respect who's already experiencing what you're after, find out what questions they habitually ask themselves to achieve those experiences, then use those questions yourself.

This is a globally powerful approach to success that can get you the things you want more quickly than anything else I've discovered. The habitual questions that others ask themselves when asked by yourself, to yourself can transform your life. You don't even need to understand how it all works really, although the answer's quite simple:

"When you change your habitual questions, you change your beliefs, when you change your beliefs, you change your actions, when you change your actions you change your results."

ClaimYourDestiny.global #ConsciousLeadership

Try it! Take the time to prove to yourself that it works, that it can change the level of pain and pleasure in your life. If you like the results, keep using the questions you've discovered until they become second nature. Do this and you won't care about the why's and the wherefore's. You'll be too busy! You'll have learned firsthand there's nothing more powerful than a good question followed by action.

Ask different questions, and you will end up thinking different thoughts, saying different words, taking different actions, and getting different results. When you go one step further by modeling the questions of successful people, you're helping to ensure that the different results you're pursuing are also good results. In other words, you've done everything you can to arrive at a different place — a good place — to develop different beliefs, which are also profitable beliefs, and to become a different person who is more like the people you admire.

FOCUS

So what does all this mean really?

It means that by looking at why you do what you do and the beliefs behind that, you can basically change the thoughts and motives that direct your behaviour so that you achieve a different result, start a new job, get a promotion, create your own business, leave a relationship, start a relationship, have that difficult conversation, learn to swim, fly a plane, or simply eat a new food; the list is endless.

It is your choice completely — where your focus goes your energy flows — so change your focus to change your results.

Some of our important choices have a timeline. If you delay a decision, the opportunity is gone forever. Sometimes your doubts will stop you from making a choice that involves change and an opportunity may be missed. If you really truly want to change, start now — now is as good a time as any.

Create and ClaimYourDestiny.global through #ConsciousLeadership

My Facebook page and group is ClaimYourDestiny or you can follow me on Twitter @JulieHogbin. Visit ClaimYourDestiny.global for more articles and up to date information, plus various other social media channels and Linkedin. My hashtag is #ConsciousLeadership if you would like to find me.

There are seven days in the week and someday isn't one of them!

ClaimYourDestiny.global
@JulieHogbin
#ConsciousLeadership

Motives and motivation are a matter of choice — yours! Choose well, look at why you believe what you believe, and question it. Listen to the answers of the questions you ask and you will create a different future if you really want to.

My final questions to you are:

• How much do you want to change?

• How willing are you to do what is required?

• What do you need to do right now?

Good luck with whatever it is you want to do. Here's to your fabulous success; you know where to find me.

Julie xx

Unstoppable

The Art of Striving

DEREK G. CHAN

HOW TO BE UNSTOPPABLE

It has been said that in order to obtain a goal, one must first see it in the mind. The child who decides he wants a cookie from the jar that's high up on the shelf or the person who wants to make partner in the law firm where they now work—each uses the same mechanism or mindset. They understand at a visceral level that you become what you think about.

The difference between the student who can break boards with their hands and feet and the one who can't, isn't skill—it's all mindset, the belief, the deep-seated knowledge that one can do it.

Golf is an interesting game. The person who can best remember the components of a good swing AND can also envision them is the one who will hit the ball far, true and straight. So it is with martial arts: you must develop a set of beliefs or a mindset that will allow you to become unstoppable. Your approach needs to be holistic in nature.

Definition of Holistic: relating to or concerned with wholes or with complete systems rather than with the analysis of, treatment of, or dissection into parts

- Holistic medicine attempts to treat both the mind and the body
- Holistic ecology views humans and the environment as a single system

At Ko Fung Martial Art, we train body, mind and soul, integrating the three elements into a holistic mindset that will make you unstoppable in life.

One of my students, Lesia Rogers, had this to say about our "wellness" approach:

Sifu Derek has truly been a blessing to me, and I am extremely grateful. It has been a year this month since he took me under his wing to teach me how first to love myself. I've also been given many tools through martial art training, coaching and nutrition.

When I first started with Derek, I was already training with someone in Tai Chi, but I'd always wanted to learn self-defence and was looking for a different martial art. Interestingly, the first thing Derek coached me to do was slow down, something I still struggle with to this day.

In the beginning, I was extremely scared and hesitant, but Derek maintained a strong awareness and was always sensitive to my needs. This was important to me as I am an emotional person and needed to reset my mindset to love, acceptance, trust, building confidence and not being afraid of life. He spent hours with me and was by my side through the thick and thin of my life (my accomplishments and my challenges). It has not been an easy journey.

I learned that it takes time for change to happen, that it requires belief in ourselves, and through coaching and training Derek has given me the beautiful gift of awareness of who I really am and what I really want in life. He's made me realize anything is possible if I truly want it. For example, I spent five years with other trainers struggling with little change in my WEIGHT. The first thing Derek did was teach me about mindset to help me understand what it takes to achieve my weight loss goal. By slowing down, listening, AND DOING, I was able to lose 10 pounds in less than two months.

Most recently he has taught me that we often face challenges in life that we have no control over. With the sudden loss of my husband, he has taught me by being there for me that life must go on. In fact, if it wasn't for Derek in the past year, I wouldn't have been prepared to deal with this sudden loss and the corresponding changes in my life.

Change is very scary and can happen suddenly. Although nobody is ever really prepared for tragedy, we must move on and take back control of our lives. Derek has been very supportive and has taught me about acceptance, redirecting and letting go with everything we do in life.

I am a stronger person than I was a year ago when we first started. Thank you to Derek. I know I would be worse off without his coaching.

I had no idea how disciplined martial art can be until I met Derek and learned his way of life. And even though I am now alone (we are never really alone), I am beginning to fill the empty space within by learning to be by myself and love myself truly.

Grateful for every moment and every breath I take, thank you, Sifu Derek.

As mentioned, martial arts represent a pathway to developing a mindset that allows you to be unstoppable. I'll provide a holistic approach to developing this mindset in your own life and give you the tools to deal with hard times whenever you encounter them. You'll learn about martial arts principles and how to apply them to your daily living. Being unstoppable is not about fearlessness or strength, but about recognizing fear and still moving forward.

In training, a martial artist gets used to regular defeats and, in turn, sees them as an opportunity to learn. Tou Lou (martial art routine) or the forms in martial arts teaches us progression. One sequence of movements leads to another. You must learn each fundamental movement first before you can move to the next sequence of movements. This structured type of learning and milestone-based achievement is valuable in all aspects of life.

Wing Chun, in particular, is an effective tool to prepare those who practice it for real life. It does so by developing skills necessary for when one encounters difficult situations. Its concepts and principles are particularly enlightening when properly interpreted and digested under a good Sifu's guidance. Form in the Wing Chun system teaches the practitioner—Awareness, Body Structure, Balance, Body Mechanics and Relaxation. Technique drills or single drills in the Wing Chun system teach the individual how to use those principles during a confrontation.

An essential aspect of having an unstoppable mindset is the ability to make timely decisions in stressful and ambiguous situations. A decision may be either right or wrong, but it's crucial to remember that far worse than an incorrect decision is a situation where no decision is made when one is necessary. Through a variety of cooperative and semi-cooperative drills, a Wing Chun practitioner is able to develop intuition, reflexes and decision-making skills while under pressure.

An example of a Wing Chun drill that develops these skills is the famous 'Chi Sao' (sticking hand) training. It is a two-person tactile sensitivity drill. One only does the attacking while the other is only defending. The objective of the attacker is learning how to use leverage, distance, angle and openings to create a successful attack. At the same time, the defender is learning how to maintain proper body structure, relaxation and counter movements while under pressure with unplanned attacks. The key to Chi Sao is accepting the force coming in (relaxation) instead of using force against force.

This develops decision-making skills through checking assumptions against facts, and develops problem-solving skills by making its practitioners consider the possible impact of their decisions throughout the process of the drill. This gives the two practitioners an opportunity to test their strengths and weakness while promoting unique and unplanned learning processes to occur.

POWER OF BREATH - STRESS MANAGEMENT

A crucial concept in Wing Chun is that of proper breathing. Siu Nim Tao is the first open hand form from the Wing Chun system and is a form of breathing meditation. Siu Nim Tao translates to "Little Idea," meaning everything starts with a thought. Without proper breathing, movement becomes stilted and ineffective. Proper abdominal breathing is a skill that is crucial for a healthier and stronger body and also for focus, which is why it is one of the first things taught.

In addition to the health and training benefits of breathing, it can also be used as an important tool for stress management. Breathing has both voluntary and involuntary control mechanisms. You can shift from being its pilot to allowing it to be left on autopilot. The voluntary aspect of breathing is what allows us to tap into its stress-managing potential.

Breathing exercises act as a form of meditation in Chinese Martial Arts. Proper abdominal breathing used in this type of meditation allows a greater volume of breath and leads to a decrease in activity of stress markers and blood levels of stress hormones.

Oftentimes, when our life is stressed, the integrity of our automatic breathing suffers. Taking advantage of the control we can exert on breathing allows us to combat stress. Learning to control our breathing can allow us to begin to control other parts of our body as well. The mind-body connection developed through breathing exercises not only physically improves our breathing but can also increase self-awareness. When you bring your body and mind in tune, your mental state will be much improved, and less susceptible to stress.

BODY STRUCTURE

Martial arts teach the skills of how to use your body structure to your advantage, and offers understanding on how the body's structure works in terms of structural alignment, the linkage of the joints, and also how simple geometry and physics can be applied to the body. A central focus of Wing Chun is adopting particular stances and postures as a framework from which to launch attacks and counter-attacks. Doing this without good posture will greatly limit your ability to be effective. In fact, your Wing Chun techniques won't be as effective unless your body is aligned correctly. This alignment also reinforces the important concept of breathing and can directly impact your ability to draw and use your breath.

Good posture means that the body is aligned with gravity, walks tall and moves with freedom in the joints. Posture in martial arts is vitally important.

This is the reason most martial arts emphasize structure from the beginning. Physical structure from a Kung Fu point of view involves a little more than just good posture, though. In addition to good posture, it adds internal connections such that your entire body learns to move as a single fluid and powerful unit.

The efficient way to get a feel for a student's structure is through single drills, Chi Sao and sparring. Good structure can be almost invisible—even to the trained eye. However, the lack of it can usually be felt as soon as contact is made with your opponent. If an opponent has good structure, a lot of techniques you could try are unlikely to work, but if their structure is poor or non-existent, almost anything you do will be effective.

What exactly is good structure and why is it so important? To put it in simple terms, good structure is the way in which you connect the different parts of yourself together internally so that they are aligned with the forces acting on your body. In Wing Chun principle and theory, the curves of the spine should be aligned, eliminating as much curvature as much as possible. It's done by tucking in the chin backward and slightly scooping forward the tailbone to avoid an anterior pelvic title. Shoulders should be relaxed and dropping with the body. By doing so, the body is able to absorb and deliver a force as one bodily unit.

The majority of people are completely disconnected and don't have proper alignment and coordination with their body. Their arms will do one thing, their legs something different, with hips only being vaguely involved. When the body does so many different things, it's impossible to connect the breath or the mind to what it's doing. This results in internal chaos and a feeling that you lack the resources to cope with your physical situation. The truth is, you don't lack the resources at all; you've just scattered them. The key to good structure is in learning how to gather all the parts of yourself together so that you can put everything you are into everything you do.

Good structure connects your arms and legs together through your centre and involves your breath working in harmony with your movements. Most importantly, the whole process is controlled by your mind, which stays focused on what you're doing. When you're connected internally, every movement involves your whole body. This internal structure can easily be felt. For example, when you try to move someone's arm who is well connected internally, you can feel that in trying to move their arm you are moving the weight of their whole body.

RELAXATION

Relaxation is a great example taught in martial arts that can easily be applied to everyday life. To be relaxed is to be natural. It should be like pouring water into your cup without any muscle tension. To get a better understanding of how to apply this in daily life, we remember how relaxation, in the context of martial arts, is supposed to be understood.

When I teach Wing Chun, I like to begin by emphasizing to my students that, in training, techniques are performed in a relaxed manner. This occurs both during training and in actual combat. In order to develop force, one must be able to relax. Why? The equation for force is mass multiplied by acceleration, and if there's any sort of muscle tension, it will only slow down the acceleration. I tend to use an analogy of a car. In order for a car to move smoothly, you will have to step on the accelerator. Step on the brake and accelerator at the same time, and it will feel like you're getting a lot of power, but in reality, you're not going anywhere.

If the arm is tensed, maximum punching speed cannot be achieved. To begin a punching motion, the arm must, in essence, first be relaxed. If relaxed at the onset, the punching may begin at any time. It is a fact that one motion is always faster than two. If there is unnecessary tension, energy will be wasted, and this will, in turn, create fatigue. In an extended engagement, this can be critical. Tension stiffens your body and thus reduces your ability to sense and react to your opponent's intentions. Look at the sport of boxing. The best boxers don't get tired—even after 12 rounds. A huge part of this is that they don't waste energy on inefficient movement. Less experienced boxers may look good early in a fight, but they often crumble in the later rounds due to not being relaxed.

I will now paraphrase two of the core points of this lesson:
  1. **Tense muscle slows down your reaction speed.**
  2. **Unnecessary tension wastes energy, causing fatigue.**

If you're overcome by anger or are tense, your mind faces identical effects and, consequently, you'll have difficulty acting with the speed you need. This unnecessary tension in your mind doesn't only waste your energy and time, it also creates a lot of undesired situations that will now need to be solved. A person with a relaxed mind can always see things more clearly than a quick-tempered person. Thus, they can easily react with proper speed and attitude. This is why a person who understands the principle of relaxation correctly can certainly be more careful and successful; they react only when necessary by keeping calm and relaxed.

BALANCE

Balance is important to all martial arts, and especially Wing Chun. It's a concept that ties together both relaxation and structure. Without balance you can't maintain structure, nor can you be relaxed as you'll always be fighting to adjust yourself and the structure you've moved away from.

The Merriam-Webster dictionary defines balance as follows:

bal·ance noun \ba-lən(t)s
- The state of having your weight spread equally so that you do not fall
- The ability to move or to remain in a position without losing control or falling
- A state in which different things occur in equal or proper amounts or have an equal or proper amount of importance

Balance in Kung Fu is often associated with the physical sense of the word. I teach my students from the day they walk in how to understand their bodies in order to develop the balance necessary to perform the forms and techniques in Wing Chun. However, physical balance isn't the only form of balance a martial arts student should learn to hone. Balance in Wing Chun isn't only about your own physical body, but understanding how to create balance between two individuals. The highest level in the art of Wing Chun isn't about how to destroy or how to inflict the most pain in an individual, but how to neutralize and balance an opponent's incoming force without harming them, and at the same time preventing them from hurting you.

"The best battle is the one that has not been fought."
- Sun Tzu

This is one of the other reasons why in Wing Chun we'll focus heavily on Chi-Sao, as it helps us understand how to find balance between two individuals—either by changing to a different position or stepping in a different angle. This is one of the skills that's transferable to everyday life and relationship-building.

There is a saying that Wing Chun Kung Fu is easy to learn but hard to master. One reason is that, in the Wing Chun system, there's a fine balance between each movement and technique. Each movement needs to be precise. There can't be any gray area as it could be a matter of your life or death in a physical confrontation. In order to find the fine balance, though, one must understand not what to do but what not to do.

Understanding this concept will also help you find balance with your overall well-being and health. It's not about knowing what type of workout we should be doing or what type of food we should eat, but what we should not be doing or eating on a daily basis. Example: all rigorous physical activity can wear down the body, and you can feel tired, sore or injured. One must always balance training and rest, and in the case of an injury, you must listen to your body. Training when too fatigued or coming back too soon from an injury can set your training back by keeping you out even more in the long run.

ROOTING AND CENTRALIZATION

"When you have roots there is no reason to fear the wind."
- Chinese Proverb

In order to understand how to become unstoppable in classical martial arts training you must recognize that it all begins with the foundation. So what does the foundation include? Strengthening the lower body by lowering your center of gravity and widening up your base. Learning how to align your skeletal structure at the same time as relaxing your body. If we're able to be rooted to the ground and our body is up straight, it's most likely going to be harder to be pushed out of balance. You can try this when you are taking the bus or subway.

1. **Imagine your head is being slightly pulled up.**
2. **Widen your base (knees are a shoulder width apart).**
3. **Slightly bend your knees to lower your center of gravity.**

You'll automatically feel more balanced and centered. A solid base is required in order for you to grow your skills and techniques. It's the same in life. It's important to understand what keeps you grounded, to discover both your values and your beliefs. By doing so, you're able to hold your ground no matter what conditions life gives you.

By being grounded, you'll eliminate fear and find inner peace. This happens as you gain the courage and strength to overcome whatever fears you might have. Training in the martial arts will always push you to your limits. It tests not only your physical strength but your mental strength as well. Know this: each time you're ready to give up, you're facing a true test of willpower. You push yourself to the limit to see how much more you can take and to see how much more you're willing to go through in order to achieve your goal. This mental strength develops into an unbreakable warrior spirit, giving you the courage to persevere through your darkest hours.

ACCEPTANCE AND LETTING GO

At a certain point in your training the ability to 'let go' becomes essential. The concept of letting go functions on two levels—physical and mental. To be able to truly let go, the physical, mental (includes emotional) aspects must function in unison.

Physically you learn to relax and release your muscles, tendons and ligaments. When you do this, it leads to the deepening of one's root and the ability to ground a powerful incoming force. In terms of meditation, this means relaxing as much as possible and 'trusting' the Earth to hold you up.

The emotional and mental aspects of 'letting go' are intertwined, meaning that emotions can trigger thought patterns, and certain thought patterns can trigger emotions. You should look for evenness and balance in your emotion. This is a non-reactive state rather than an absence of emotion per se. This emotional neutrality is like a placid lake that appears to be a mirror. In this state, it becomes possible to read a person's true emotional intention like an open book.

For the mind, you want, at first, a gentle calmness and a slowing of thought, but this eventually develops into what has been termed 'mind of no mind.' This mind of no mind is actually an optimal state for both the meditative aspect as well as the martial. For meditation, we can perceive and become aware of things without the mind's judgement. In martial arts, this 'mind of no mind' state is optimal for success in combat. When centered in such a state you are able to act or react at a speed that can be faster than the speed of thought!

Accepting and letting go are probably two of the hardest things to do. Whether it's a relationship, anger from an argument or simply past mistakes; instead of being stuck in the moment, accept the emotion and the situation with your arms wide open. Acknowledge, embrace and let go. Let go of emotions and situations that don't serve you as a whole or lead you to greater things. It's beyond whether you were right or wrong. It's about setting yourself free. It begins with the willingness to accept ourselves exactly as we are, right where we are, with no judgements or preconceived notions. For the martial element, you must go even further. Instead of fearing an opponent's attack, you must learn to welcome it. This is all a matter of lack of tension. Therefore, the stronger an attack, the more relaxed you must initially become to deal with it. This method is grounded in a Wing Chun principle that states, "Accept what comes, escort what leaves." By accepting the incoming force, it will enable you to reposition and let go of what's coming in at you.

Once this is accomplished you no longer react to circumstances as average people do. Instead, you find yourself centered and alert—ready to deal with a situation without having your natural adrenal reaction getting in the way. This is not only supremely useful in combat but also in your daily life.

MOVING FORWARD

"Your one-step back is your opponent's two-step forward."
–Derek G. Chan

One of the most important rules of Wing Chun is that you don't step back. It is structure that gives us the advantage over the larger opponent, and when we become our worst enemy by destroying our own structure, it's not too difficult to predict the outcome of a fight. While Wing Chun may have backward stepping and backward bracing, these footworks are not designed for you to initiate. In Wing Chun we always move forward; only when the force dictates it do we actually move backwards. Footwork in Wing Chun is always taking you forward. It might be in a direct straight line or at an angle, but it allows you to swallow up any space that opens up between you and an attacker, limiting their options and overwhelming them.

Some of the most skilful boxers are those that can deliver a knockout blow while going backwards. While this may be much to the appreciation of the crowd, Wing Chun has no time for any of this. The footwork drives you forward all the time. One of the most important rules I always remind my students of during our sparring sessions is to continue to move forward—mentally and physically. It's important to create opportunities either by footwork, by stepping in a different angle, or a follow-up technique. There may be times when it is best to be stationary and wait for the perfect timing and openings. However, if you are against a more experienced opponent, the only chance of you overcoming the situation is by closing the distance and creating the opening. If you don't, not only do you have a lesser chance of winning, you're also leaving yourself vulnerable as a stationary target.

By having the attitude of forward movement, it will greatly benefit you in your daily life. Life is your experienced and stronger opponent. It doesn't matter how organized or how well-planned you are; life will always throw obstacles at you. In order for you to conquer them, you must start by moving forward. If you keep waiting for the perfect time or the perfect day, you'll never get anything done, and, sadly, you'll also miss a lot of opportunities. Instead, start moving forward and create your own path, regardless of how tough the situation is. If there's a will there is a way.

FOCUS

It can take a continuous daily effort to reach your goals. However, focusing on your long-term expectations, you'll find the strength to keep going even in the face of temporary setbacks. Those trained in Wing Chun will tell you that in the process you'll face a lot of challenges and setbacks. The students who are able to recognize that such setbacks are necessary hurdles and pitfalls they must navigate along the path to their destination are also the ones who succeed. Without that realization a student faces great difficulty overcoming those setbacks because they may lose sight of their long-term goals and allow themselves to get lost, joining the many casualties who fall by the wayside.

To focus, you must not only find a goal but also envision and look beyond at what lies ahead. The same principle applies to Karate practitioners when they attempt to break boards. If they only focus on the surface, their success rate of breaking the boards decreases as their force will be slowed down before they reach the target. However, if they are envisioning and telling themselves to hit behind or through the boards, the chance of them breaking the board is a lot higher.

Life is a series of experiences. There will be times where you're stuck in the moment. Whether it's a failure in a business partnership or the loss of a family member, it's up to you to endure and envision what lies ahead and continue to march forward. By doing so, you'll develop a stronger self and character. This is what separates those who are short-sighted from those who are long-sighted.

TECHNIQUE—EFFICIENT AND ECONOMICAL

"Offence is Defence, Defence is Offence."
- Wing Chun Proverb

One of Wing Chun's unique points is that it doesn't rely on any brute strength to overcome an adversary. We'll always place ourselves as the fragile person. Why? There will always be someone bigger, stronger and faster. And the way to overcome a larger assailant is by understanding the power of proper body structure and relaxation.

To become more efficient and economical with your movements, you'll defend and attack simultaneously. Doing so will allow you to become more efficient with your movements. One example is the Lap Da or Lap Sao technique. This is a technique where one hand sinks the opponent's straight attack while your other hand punches. In order to execute these fine movements, there will be an emphasis on body coordination drills. Without being coordinated, you wouldn't have the ability to execute the technique as smoothly. Wing Chun techniques often require you to have your hands and lower body cooperating with one another. Being well coordinated also means one is well-balanced. As human beings, we already apply the principle of balance while we are walking, our left hand will swing out, right foot steps forward, and vice versa. However, as a martial artist sometimes we tend to forget about this basic principle, and we think martial arts movements and everyday movements are two separate entities.

Having the Wing Chun mindset of being efficient will change our approach to handling daily tasks. It will help us realize how important it is to utilize our energy more efficiently (as it will help us manage time). In Wing Chun philosophy, time is an important factor. For this reason, each movement and technique has to be precise. As it could be a matter of life or death if you're in a confrontation. Every inch, every angle, every movement comes into play. Wing Chun is a system that does not discriminate, as it is not about who is bigger, stronger and faster. It's about understanding how to utilize proper body mechanics and physics to your advantage. It's understanding how to execute the most impactful thing efficiently and effectively in the limited time and energy you're given. This is why, in classical martial arts, you'll strike on vital spots and soft tissues on the opponent when placed in a life or death situation. By embracing this Wing Chun concept, you're able to focus more and utilize your time and energy more efficiently and effectively in your regular daily routine.

To learn more about Derek's method of Wing Chun visit us at
www.kofung.ca or contact us at info@kofung.ca

Five Key Elements for Success

Shift to the Next Level

ALANA LEONE

There are moments in our lives when we have an opportunity to change our path, to explore in a new direction, and to step out into the unknown. Too often, doubts and fears can take hold in our lives, limiting the risks we take and the amount of success we can claim.

I want you to change all that. I don't offer this lightly. With the power of opening your mind to peak performance thinking, you are putting yourself on the path to generate the success you want in your life.

Now, to be clear, all of us have different definitions of success. You are already successful now in some areas of your life. Now let's take that to the next level.

It involves laser focusing on what you want instead of being stuck with what you don't want. By creating a drive to pursue your desires and ditching your limiting decisions and beliefs, your life will take on a whole new meaning. You leave the plateau and reach new heights. You feel energized! It takes stepping outside of your comfort zone and overcoming challenges instead of creating obstacles. It takes climbing one step at a time to the next peak.

As part of my work, I assist people to make the transition away from their fixed thinking and their inability to take advantage of the possibilities around them. Instead, I invite them to open their minds and explore what success they can claim through a shift to next level thinking. I give them the strategies, tools, and behaviors to be able to do it themselves.

Part of a mindset shift involves removing the sting of failure. I often tell my grandson, "What a lie of the mind it is to think you are going to start something brand new and you are not going to fail."

It is what you do with the failure that gets you to the next peak or leaves you stuck on the plateau. Take what you learn, implement it, and then do it again. When you take failure as feedback, it becomes less personal. If it is something you have decided you want, you will do it. Look at when you first learned to drive. Did you fail? If you are like me, then you likely did fail every day until the day you didn't. I didn't quit. You likely didn't either. I took what I learned and got back behind the wheel. This process is a strategy for success. It's a tool you already used in other areas of your life — only, you forgot.

Your mind likes to put you down and keep you safe. Mine too! Now I say thank you to my mind and make a shift to the next level. I have control over my mind, not the other way around. Too often, we attach negative emotions to failure. Instead, recognize it as a positive learning experience, one that is meant to assist your growth. There is potential in all of us to change, to alter ourselves and our circumstances. Too often, we allow our circumstances to turn into a much bigger obstacle, one that quickly becomes a blockade in achieving our goals and desires.

How can you push through the blockade? First, determine whether you are thinking with a fixed mindset or an open, curious one. As you explore your thinking patterns, you will be able to blast through the obstacles and blockades your mind has created.

As part of this journey, I am going to share with you the importance of five key elements for success. You can achieve success with these elements just by taking one step, then another — to shift to the next level.

PUSH THROUGH TO SUCCESS

When you operate with a fixed mindset, there arc a few elements that come into play. One of the first is how you talk to yourself. In a fixed mindset, your self-talk tends to have a negative aspect to it. Time and again, you tell yourself that was a stupid decision. , You ask yourself "Why did you think you could do that?" or "Don't take the risk!" There is a lot of "No, no" and "Wait, wait" throughout that list.

Plus, when your self-talk is full of negativity, and on a constant repeat, then you quickly begin to believe what you are telling yourself. A vicious cycle starts, one that cannot stop unless you make a conscious effort to do so.

That self-talk also impacts your reality. After all, if you think you are not capable, then your subconscious mind is going to seek out the evidence of that from your surroundings. It reinforces that negativity.

Your subconscious mind is listening to the words you say. It believes that these words are what you want. That is why I cannot say it enough: Think and say what you want, not what you don't want. I catch myself doing this all the time. I frequently ask myself, "Is that what I want? If not, then change it right now!" Once you spend time focused on the positive or what you want, then you will see it leak out of your mind through your mouth. Then it moves from your mouth to your actions. It is a beautiful sight and sound. Once you experience it over and over, you feel amazing.

When you push through a negative mindset, you make the conscious choice to focus your thoughts around a positive viewpoint. There are many tools for your toolbox in the world today, and you have to be willing to use them. You gain the discipline to keep on top of it. Look at football or any sport you love. The coach is there every game and every practice to push through negative mindsets and motivate the team. The coach doesn't come at the first part of the year to give the team a pep talk and then nothing the rest of the year! He constantly pushes and reminds the team, "You got this!"

How can you make these new decisions? The first part of any new strategy is recognizing what decisions to eliminate. Recognize that eliminating one negative decision or belief means another positive decision of belief must replace it. Otherwise, within the vacuum, your old ways are likely to return.

Next level thinking is about pushing yourself to identify those unproductive patterns within your subconscious way of thinking and shifting them into what you desire. Often the best way to address limiting decisions and beliefs is through a conscious dig into your past.

Past experiences and decisions create limiting decisions and beliefs. In turn, that past creates a root cause, likely within the years of your life up to age seven. In fact, without learning from the past issues, you are susceptible to another limiting decision or belief based on the same root cause. Think of a tree with lots of fruit on it. You automatically assume that the roots of the tree are flourishing. However, there may be rot that is not visible to the naked eye. The same is true of your life. There may be root causes that keep you from flourishing but are not easily spotted.

Let's start with examining what root causes are and how to tear out those rotting roots and replace them with nourished, healthy roots for your life and your business.

ELEMENT #1 - ROOT CAUSES

First, let's start with how you are thinking now and the impact it has on your life.

We all have a story that starts with detailed events and ends pointing the finger at someone else, declaring them guilty of some misdeed. In many ways, this is the story of self. What you believe about yourself and others in your story gets ingrained further through a spiral of negative thoughts and actions.

The more we talk about this, the deeper it gets driven. At some point, the body starts to feel the emotions in other ways, such as sickness, depression, rage, and anxiety. A trip to the doctor for a pharmaceutical cure focuses on the ailing body, but not the root cause in the spirit.

As you think back to the main events of your story, I would like you to come up with an age when an event occurred. Are you two, four, six, ten or twelve? Now I would like you to think about how long you have been preparing and restructuring this story of the past into your conceptualized self. This part creates an identity. There is usually a lot of emotional baggage, often sadness, anger, fear, hurt, and guilt. You end up feeling trapped and making decisions based on those emotions. Thus, you create a pattern of self-sabotage or procrastination. You want the procrastination to go away, but it goes much deeper than just procrastination. The cause is deep in the soil and the roots, corroding and rotting them further.

It becomes a deadweight in your life, one that keeps you from pushing forward. How long do you want to be trapped by those emotions, the hurts, and the negative energy that comes from these stories in your life? How long is enough for you to hurt before you are done with it? When do you decide that it is time for you to have the freedom to push forward?

Our childhoods are not dictated by us, but by the people who surround us. Parents, extended family, and others impact who we are and the experiences that we have. Those experiences shape our beliefs about ourselves and who we are in the world. However, there are also those of us who grow up in situations based on past hurts. Those older adults do not know how to address their past hurts, so they pass those hurts onto their children. It becomes a generational hurt, one that has roots so deep it can be hard even to address them.

They have all done the best they can with their experiences. This reality may be hard to hear, and it doesn't give people a pass for being this way. However, they were that way, and now it is up to you to push forward and make different choices because you can see a different path. The best thing you could do to get back at them is to have massive success and joy.

Let the events in your past propel you to impact your present and future for good. You might want to break that cycle of negativity and rot. However, that can be difficult because you don't know any other way to think, feel, or behave. What do you do?

Our society is changing, and the next generations are determined not to carry that heavy emotional and mental baggage into the future. Their choice to address these issues or root causes means developing new tools. My passion is to share these tools with others for the next generations and our nations, thus transforming our world with information and education.

One aspect of shifting our thinking is in recognizing new teachings about how to harness the power of your mind. Some people were taught about the mind, how powerful it is, and how it helps to keep us safe. Some people were taught that we have control over the actions of our mind. We are not powerless over our thoughts. You are programmed with certain beliefs and values. The good news is, if you want to change the old programming, then you can.

Shifting your negative beliefs and useless values can take courage. In the end, however, it is a very cleansing experience. By that I mean, when you settle past hurts, you can address your emotional baggage and set it down for good. How can you set that past baggage down?

Part of that is based around the principle of forgiveness. When you forgive someone, you free yourself from any power they might have over you, mentally and emotionally. Forgiveness involves letting go of any resentment and refusing to allow them to hold you emotionally hostage. Often, while you might be hurting, they might not even still be thinking of you or even remember the hurt that they caused. That person might even justify it in their minds, believing that it was for your good.

In the end, you have the power to decide how long you are willing to let the actions of others impact you. It is up to you now to take responsibility in your choice to stay stuck or push forward. It is not always easy to make that decision and stick with it. Emotions can come into play, essentially sabotaging your efforts. When you choose a path and stick with it, then you find that shift in your thinking. The most effective way is to remove the emotion around the event and come up with some learnings. This process is what I have mastered. Do not let your mind come up with excuses. Rid yourself of the past burdens and fly free.

My passion is to give people tools to clear those emotions. It is important to remove the toxic negative emotion — the root cause — by filling your roots with a powerful positive emotion. You need to give yourself the tools to drain the emotion of a memory. Doing so will allow you to be at peace with those events and then push forward with your life.

Another important point is that you can have positive root causes as well. Those are the memories and emotional ties that helped you understand your purpose or gave you a belief system that continues to support you.

Positive roots can also be a way to connect with others. When you have a positive experience, it tends to color your day and make you more inclined to try and do the same for others. Shifting your thinking involves taking those positive root experiences and allowing them to help you gain a deeper understanding of yourself and to deal with others in a kind, generous, and loving way.

I love the metaphor of the tree. Roots are so critical to the life of the tree. Without proper care, then the tree will eventually die from a lack of food, water, and stability. Think of all the ways that your roots provide stability in your life. They ground you, give you a sense of the world you live in, and social rules that help you to operate in that world. Negative root causes can be damaging to your internal root system, thus threatening your stability and the means by which you can continue to grow and flourish in your life. Granted, it is possible to save the tree, but that means you need to do the hard work to address the rot. Addressing rot involves self-care and hard work, as well as creating new patterns that will nourish healthy roots.

Essentially, addressing rot can save the tree. Plus, when you take the time to care for your roots, both positive and negative, then you will find that your tree is healthier and more stable.

When you see a tree with toxic roots — the leaves are brown and sparse — there is evidence of compromised stability. It is dying a slow painful death. After some time, the tree will fall over in a windstorm. Move to a picture of a tall, healthy tree with strong roots. This tree will have a lot of leaves and be strong and confident in its stature. It will also have big, juicy, and excellent tasting fruit, and live a long, healthy life.

The healthier the roots, the more productive the tree and the more excellent the fruit. Your life can be the one you have always imagined, but only if you are willing to change how you interact with the world by addressing the various root causes within your background. I want you to be a healthy tree, not one with sparse and brown leaves, struggling to survive the windstorms of life.

Now you need to look at your roots. Are they healthy or can you detect some signs of rot? When you detect that rot, it is important to address it right away. Next level thinking means not allowing thoughts, emotions, and events to fester and cause further damage. At the same time, when you address those root causes, then you are dealing with the damage already done.

I want you to understand that it is possible to get your roots healthy and keep you growing and thriving. Next level thinking focuses on helping you understand yourself better, including why you react a certain way, and why certain situations trigger specific emotions. There are always root causes.

Addressing them will help clear the way to change how you react not only in these situations but in other stressful circumstances and wind storms.

I am passionate about helping individuals detect the rot in their roots and then ferret it out. Once you clear the damaged roots, the tree (you) can flourish and grow toward your goals and dreams without that dead weight. Part of that process is not only clearing the negative, but also helping new roots grow in place of those old roots.

Too often, people focus on those old root causes and make them the obstacle that keeps them from pushing forward and embracing new ways of thinking. However, when you decide that you will address those root causes and that they will no longer be obstacles, then you can begin to see the new possibilities that await you! You begin to look for new roots.

Recap:
- Root causes impact our beliefs and values, how we think, and our self-talk.
- Addressing root causes can leave room for new growth.
- Work with me to clear out your rot and clear the obstacles in your path.

ELEMENT #2 - NEW ROOTS

To be even more successful, you need to recognize the responsibility you have in your life to choose change. You are in charge and have the power to shift your beliefs and values. Your experiences give you valuable learnings, so you can reach out to expand and flourish. Your mindset controls your behavior. When you take the knowledge and leave behind the emotional sabotage, you will train your brain to search and keep busy looking for positive information.

It is like a puppy that is full of energy. When you aren't giving the puppy something productive to do, then it will eat your shoes. Keep your mind busy with actionable thoughts and productivity, thus training it to work for you and find even more creative ways to keep busy. Your mind will spiral up and not down. Give your mind something powerful to focus on.

Shifting your thinking can help you transition into the type of thinking that will allow you to envision a new path for yourself and then work to achieve that change. To have more success in all areas of your life, you need to recognize that you and only you have the responsibility of choice — and to change your environment. You are the one that has to move your foot forward to take that step.

I can help you decide where you want to place your foot, but you need to be the one to take that step. As you create new roots for yourself, it will be easier to push forward. Recognize that you are teaching yourself a new skill, one that is going to require you to step outside of your comfort zone. Like any new skill, it might feel awkward at first, but over time that awkwardness will fade.

I want you to stop for a moment and think about the language you use when trying to do something new. There are phrases that you can use which will indicate how successful you can be. When you start with a negative mindset and speak negatively about what you are attempting, then you are likely to find yourself giving up if it is not successful on the first try.

Too often, people focus on what they are doing wrong or they ask "why questions." For example, "Why does this happen to me?" Notice when you shift your mindset and start to create new strategies and processes, you begin to look at what you are doing that is amazing. Then you might start asking yourself, "How do I focus on expanding that positive energy?" Positive thoughts and energy attract more positive thoughts and energy.

Now, shift that language to more positive language. Do you see the difference in how willing you are to keep going in the face of challenges? How you talk about something and what you focus on about that item or experience can help determine if you will be successful or not. When you say, "I can get into this," it is positive. When you say, "I won't be able to get this done," it is negative. Pay attention to what you say. It is very important. The point of new roots is that you are changing your focus and how you speak about the events in your life.

I want to push you to step outside of your comfort zone and think about how you talk to yourself and how you talk out loud to others. What are you truly ordering up on the menu of life? If you are not clear and using clear, positive language, you are probably going to continue to find your goals thwarted or the delivery being less than what you had hoped to achieve. You think you are ordering a 12-course meal, yet you get back liver stew.

After taking my four years of training, I realized that I now had a skill that would help me push forward in my life and to create an amazing future for myself. I know how to talk to my goal-getter, and the results have been incredible. I want you to have the same experience. By taking the time to look at your mental language, you can find the patterns or places where communication is breaking down and create new positive processes.

It is up to you to create new roots and allow yourself to be at peace with your past, just as it was up to me to do that for myself. Once you put all the pieces into place, then the possibilities are endless.

When you are defining your new roots, you need to have a laser focus on what you want. Distraction can keep you from achieving what you want. If you find that you are distracted, remember that you do not have to stay that way!

Part of my pushy training is about pushing you to move past those distractions and to regain your focus. You have control over your thoughts. Consider your thoughts as leaves on a running river. If you are standing on the bank of the river, then you will see those leaves floating passed you. Your thoughts are also moving at the speed of a river, so you need to decide which leaf to grab.

That is how you need to focus, simply by picking one positive thought or idea and then giving it your full attention. When you focus on a pattern of negative thoughts, then you are going to find that type of energy coming your way. However, when you immediately decide to focus on the positive, then you draw that positive energy towards yourself.

Here are just a few examples of the types of positive energy that you can create with your thoughts: love, understanding, and compassion. It is about flexibility to focus and also to dream and live in a creative space.

Now that you have an understanding of how you can control your thoughts, you can identify the patterns that could be obstacles in your life. The obstacles are a tapestry of limiting decisions, negative beliefs and values, to name a few. These drive you to take action or not. If your drive in the past has allowed you to coast, then we need to push the gas pedal. Change involves making the move to throw the bags out of the trunk, thus lightening your load. Then press the accelerator to the mat and take off!

Recap:

- Shift your thinking from the negative to the positive.

- Take control of your thoughts. You have the power!

- Create a laser focus on what you desire to achieve.

Now, I want to shift your focus to the last three elements I will be discussing in this chapter.

ELEMENT #3 - PURSUE YOUR DESIRES

Align your life and business to your desires. We have looked in detail at the root causes and received the learnings and released the negative emotions from the events. We have created new roots and realizations. You are thinking about things differently and in a new light. Now you may have determined what you want and may even have a vague idea of how you are going to get there.

You may find that, now, you are ready to focus on how you are going to achieve the life you desire or even to focus on the fact that such a life is possible. Remember, use direct and clear language with yourself and others that defines a specific path. If you don't do this you might not get what you expect, even though you followed the path. Your words and phrases need to be in alignment with the possibilities. The various parts of you need to be integrated, and then you need to decide on a clear path.

As you sharpen your definition of the life you desire, you give your mind something to work with. Start by asking great questions of yourself and others. Get curious about what you like and what you don't. When you work at home, which tasks tend to go quickly, and which ones tend to drag on and on?

Define your strengths and weaknesses. They can help you see what areas might be creating challenges in your life that you need to address. How can your strengths work more effectively for you? What might you need to go learn more about to turn your weaknesses into strengths?

One of the best ways to truly define the life that you desire is to visualize yourself in the life you want today as if you already have it. Write out in a journal that ideal and desired life. Give it as many details as possible. Include what it feels like, sounds like, smells like, and looks like. See yourself there and then describe that image. Act as if it is today you have what you want. I am sure that you might have done something similar in the past, but now that you have looked at root causes, it is time to do it again. What you focus on only gets bigger as you get accustomed to taking those massive actions! Focus on the desire.

One caution about focusing on your desire is to not stay in the future all the time. It is a beautiful dance to be able to be in the present most of the time and also focused on the future at times. It is about putting the desire in the future with you in the picture and then being in the present to complete the tasks.

It is also about fun. Being in the present is fun. I will straight out start belly laughing in the middle of something, and people say, "It is her laughing time." That laughing time is catchy though, and others soon start to laugh along. It is also my process for bringing me back into the present. I enjoy floating around in the future, sometimes too often. The action happens in the present.

You want to have everything you ever dreamed of in your life. You and I only get one chance at this life. What is holding you back? What are you going to do about it? Clearly, throughout our discussion, I have identified some root causes that you need to consider, as they could be blocks. However, I have also shared a few points to help you address them. Now I want to connect with you to help you to shift your thinking and keep going on the journey at my website, www.pushycoach.com.

Recap:
- Define your desires.

- Determine what is holding you back.
- Don't stay in the future, but keep a foot in the present.

ELEMENT #4 - ACTION

All that I have talked about throughout this chapter has led to this element, the one regarding action. Too many of us focus on the fear of a situation, and that keeps us from acting. However, when you focus on what you want — I mean laser focus — that fear will go away. You will move forward, despite the fear.

You must choose your mindset. Success is a decision. Not having success is a decision as well. A positive mindset takes work. It's like working a muscle. The more you go to the gym, the bigger the muscle. The more you focus on your positive mindset, the better the chance of getting that desire. You make the desire bigger and brighter, bigger and brighter.

When you learn the pattern of clear focus, then your vision gets bigger, clearer, and brighter. Focusing on the future and then acting on that vision means you are focusing on the future and not on the past. It is a sure sign that you are growing strong roots and are ready to move forward.

When you do make strides forward and an obstacle gets in your way, or you fail at something, it could be easy to decide to quit. A lot of people quit and tell themselves, "I guess it wasn't meant to be."

Keep your power and the ability that you have to be successful. If you are starting to do something that you have never done before, why would you expect not to have obstacles or that you might not have failures along the path to success? It is unrealistic to think that way.

Put positive processes in your mind every day. Give your mind exercise. Going back to the coach story, you recognize that coaches are consistently telling you new teachings and giving you more motivation — not once, consistently! Doing small things consistently is the key.

People get busy doing tasks that have nothing to do with their desire and then the day disappears — a week, a month, a year, ten years. Act now.

Additionally, it is critical to have a support team in place to help you as you transition to your shifted life. This is why I love setting up Mastermind groups. Masterminds are where like-minded people get together to work on a clear direction and get the wisdom and experience from the entire room, not just yours alone. Who is in your support team? Think about the people you rely on for advice, encouragement, and motivation. Are they providing that or are they bringing out the negative and showcasing a critical spirit?

Recognize that to build a positive support team, you need to be willing to be a positive support to others. That quality will draw people of like-mind to you. Do not be afraid to let go of the people that are limiting you, despite your efforts to be supportive of their dreams. Perhaps letting go of that relationship will make room for greater opportunities, including the chance to meet new people who can join your inner circle.

My point is that I know you are going to achieve great things. Do you know it? Once you do achieve them, it is important to celebrate and express gratitude to help keep those positive roots nourished.

Recap:
- Take the first step to create success.
- Build a support team.
- Be supportive of others, and it will return to you!

ELEMENT #5 - CELEBRATION AND GRATITUDE

Probably the best part of achieving anything in life is the satisfaction of knowing that you accomplished what you set out to create. That can be the push you need to start a new project or create a new chapter in another area of your life. I always believe in celebrating your successes, as it can be a true source of motivation and inspiration. However, celebrations do not have to be limited to times when you accomplish something or are successful in an effort. Find at least one thing to celebrate everyday!

When I do my talks, I ask the group if they have celebrated themselves that day? I always raise my hand. My hand is often the only hand raised.

Why is this the case? You are so good at being hard on yourself that you are not good at celebrating yourself and your accomplishments. Without your struggles and obstacles, then you would not be who you are. You are an amazing individual, especially because of your blemishes and scars. Your marks say who you are, and they make you the strong person you are. That is something to celebrate.

The point is that celebrating yourself is meant to push you forward to the next level and shift your thinking to bring you the life you desire. Part of that process involves being grateful for what you have achieved already. Gratitude is something that you can pass on to others, and it creates a positive energy that only grows.

Part of celebrating yourself involves exploring what you enjoy and trying new things. When you find fun things to do, then they keep you in a great state of mind. You have the choice to create your day your way, so why not start as soon as your eyes open! Starting this way could be the most comfortable and rewarding process of your day.

Recap:

- Celebrate what you have accomplished.
- Be grateful for your abilities.
- Explore new things and step outside of your comfort zone.

SHIFTING YOUR THOUGHTS STARTS NOW!

Here is a 10-minute process for you to begin shifting your thinking first thing in the morning. Do it consistently. Before even setting your feet on the ground.

This process is known as the "Push through to your purpose" process. It is given to you from the The Pushy Coach®. I created this so that people can shift their thinking even before they put their feet on the ground first thing in the morning. When does the mind start with its noise? Right — first thing! Beat your mind and put in the shift of positive energy before your feet hit the floor. You can do this process even before you are out of bed or while you are still stirring. I call this process the easiest process because you are still in bed. You can begin to build healthy roots for your amazing life from the comfort and warmth of your own bed.

1. Decide and choose this time to not only wake up physically and emotionally, choose to wake up consciously and to live on purpose.

2. Set an intention for your day. Intentions are critical for taking action. Some examples to get you started.

   a. I am open to new positive experiences today.

   b. I experience myself of service to others today.

    c.   I am 100 percent present and aware with others today.

    d.   I experience myself healthy, wealthy, and unconditionally happy today.

3. Say three to seven gratitude statements. What are you happy about? Some examples to get you started.

    a.   I am grateful for the sun.

    b.   I am grateful for my family and/or friends.

    c.   I am grateful to have woken up this morning.

    d.   I am grateful for the fresh air today.

4. Celebrate one success from the day before.

5. Say, "I like myself. This day is the best day ever!"

6. Visualize great things happening today. Get up you amazing person.

7. Repeat the process daily.

The secret is to focus on what you want. With these few new things to do, even before you get out of bed, you will be creating a great add-on to the success elements that you are already making a part of your life.

To do something different — to break through your comfort zone barrier — is part of living your desired life. When you get proactive to your outcomes and desires and less reactive to limiting decisions, beliefs, unaligned values, and more, then you can truly move your life onto the path that allows you to have an amazing life journey.

You can say you didn't know before, but now you do know. To live and to pursue your desired life is a choice you can make or not. Taking action is a responsibility. Consider yourself pushed. If you need a bigger push, then contact me at www.pushycoach.com or ask us about our 1-year "Shift to the Next Level" coaching package and also how to get the bonus 5-hour "Breakthrough Experience".

I believe in tearing out the old roots so much that I want to get you a fresh beginning by taking the "Breakthrough Experience" before starting your Next Level Coaching to get you to the next level in your life. In the Breakthrough Experience, you can learn to release root causes, and in the "Shift to the Next Level" coaching, you can lock in new roots to pursue your desired life with action. Take action and celebrate yourself and others with gratitude.

I appreciate you, and I thank you for taking the time to read through and learn about next level thinking. With you here, it also helps me move forward to a new way of thinking. When you think about it, there is always a next level, and we can do it together.

To learn more about Alana Leone, please go to www.pushycoach.com

Nobody Got Time For That!

The Ultimate Guide For Smart Money Management

URSULA GARRETT

S ave, save, save! That's all you hear from family, friends and the media. You are strongly encouraged to save, but how are you supposed to save with a low-paying job, high student loan debt, and the rising cost of housing? Something has got to give – and it's usually not you giving to your savings account. Who has time to be broke when you are young and just want to have fun and enjoy your life? I'll tell you who – nobody. Nobody has got time for that, especially you!

Finances absolutely play a huge part in your life choices and opportunities. Money issues consume chunks of your brain power every day. Think of how many times money (or a lack of it) factors into your decisions throughout your fast-paced day. For instance, you schedule a date on Tinder, buy movie tickets on Fandango and make dinner reservation using Open Table, and you haven't even gotten out of bed yet to start your day. You can do this if you have money in your bank account or power (available credit) on your credit card. Yes, either method of payment will get you what you want right now – one is a smart choice and the other, not so much. You must make smart choices regularly, there is no getting around it.

Size does matter, especially when it refers to your bank account. I want you to recognize that money underwrites the type of life you live and the lack of it means you're not living the life you want to be living. You are forced to make hard choices about what you can afford or what you have to give up. Having limited options make you feel as if your life is less than it could be. Smart money management is the key to your financial goals and personal goals aligning.

Once you recognize that the choices you make with your finances are either limiting your options or providing you opportunities, you can start being more proactive with your finances. First, it is important for you to understand how easy it is to handle your personal business, so you can create real changes that will significantly impact your life.

Two of my five daughters are about the same age, 26 (not twins just a blended family). Throughout their lives, they have taken different paths and made different choices. They are in their mid-twenties now and both spend more than they should, however, one is contributing to a retirement plan and has money go directly from her paycheck into a savings account. The other one lives paycheck to paycheck, has no retirement savings, no personal savings, and is regularly subsidized by her parents. Three guesses which one has more opportunities to live the life she wants, and the first two guesses don't count. While they each had similar opportunities, their individual choices have dictated their current circumstances.

"I am not a product of my circumstances. I am a product of my decisions."

- Stephen Covey

It's a bit of a mystery why you make some of the decisions you make and that's especially true when it comes to your finances. I can tell you from experience that a crystal ball, mesmerizing though it may be, is not where you will find those answers. How often have you made poor financial choices in the moment, only to later regret them and wonder how you got into this situation again? Well, I'm here to tell you that it doesn't matter how or why, what matters is what you do to fix it and make sure it never happens again.

If you have ever paid attention to political elections, then you know how easily you can be fooled by your assumptions, fears and false intuitions. I say this to help you understand that listening to others' opinions about what you should do won't help you reach your goals. Making a plan and following through will.

Which is why I find it useful to understand some principle concepts when you make decisions about money. This is besides, of course, the regular practices of following a budget, saving, investing and avoiding most kinds of debt, factors that I will discuss as part of the steps for smart money management.

These four concepts are the foundation you need for your decision-making process when you are creating your budget or making the decisions about those investments and savings plans. They need to factor into all your financial decisions, because they will help keep you from sabotaging your financial stability.

1) OPPORTUNITY COSTS

No matter what you do or the opportunities that you pursue, there is always going to be a cost. You have to give something to get something. Nothing in life is free. Individually, we get to decide what we are willing to give in exchange. In some circumstances, the price is simply too high, or the payoff is too low to make the deal or take the chance. That threshold is different for everyone and is based on your values.

For example, deciding whether or not to pursue higher education is a decision you make based on your priorities, which could include your financials, your time, and your perception of the value of higher education. Pursuing an advanced degree may take years -- are you willing to put in that amount of time? It could involve giving up other opportunities to finish your degree, but at the same time, the network you build could allow you access to individuals who can create even greater career opportunities in the future. Many individuals choose their university based on the alumni and the type of network they can access for mentors.

Additionally, there is the debt that often comes with pursuing higher education. Are you willing to put yourself into that kind of debt, the type of debt that will take years to pay off? Many individuals see their degree as a doorway to career advancement in a specific field or as a way to pursue the type of work that they are passionate about. For them, the cost of the degree in terms of finances and time is worth it, because they see that degree as an investment in their long-term financial future.

Those two daughters I mentioned earlier, one went to college and has a degree in business and some student loan debt. The other worked part-time jobs and traveled to visit friends she met on the internet. One daughter wanted a college degree and was willing to sacrifice four years of her life, accumulate debt (she considered it as an investment) and forego immediate travel opportunities. The other daughter thought that price was too high. This isn't a matter of right or wrong but a matter of what you are willing to give to get what you want. Here is a general rule of thumb: The bigger the opportunity, the greater the cost or sacrifice to achieve it.

Every decision that you make has all those considerations and it is up to you to give them all a voice before you make your decision. At the same time, your priorities need to guide those smaller financial decisions that we all make throughout the day. Many of your long-term goals are going to be impacted by your short-term decisions. Therefore, giving yourself guidelines for daily spending based on your priorities will help you to reach those goals. Still, not everything can be quantified in terms of your return on investment, as I will explore next.

2) SUNK COSTS

What is sunk cost? This is money you can't get back -- a non-refundable airline ticket, for example. There are certain expenses that you will have throughout your life that are not going to bring a tangible return on investment. In fact, they are likely going to result in nothing more than an enjoyable experience or a pleasant memory. It can be easy to get into a mindset that has you spending far beyond what you may have budgeted or prioritized because you value the experience, but it can put you in a financial bind later. The idea here is that you need to keep sunk costs in proper perspective. It's easy to start thinking, "Well, I've already spent $100, so what's another $25?" My mother always told me not to throw good money after bad. She taught me to understand the concept of sunk costs long before I took a business class. You have got to be willing to walk away sometimes and keep the money in your pocket for other investment opportunities.

Once something is paid for, and cannot be refunded, it shouldn't impact your future financial decisions. It is a "sunk" cost, i.e. water under the bridge, and no matter what you do in the future you won't ever get it back. Therefore, you can't allow yourself to get hung up on the moments where you spent money in a way that didn't fall into your overall financial plan. In the end, you have to accept that sunk costs are going to happen and make your peace with them. Recognize that you will buy emotionally and defend rationally, even if that might not always be wise. There are costs that are simply not recoupable.

Regrets over sunk costs can make it harder to move forward, leaving you vulnerable to make other choices that you may not have otherwise made. Do not allow yourself to fall into the downward spiral. Negative thoughts often breed more negative thoughts, especially if you continue to dwell on them. The same can be said for financial decisions. When you focus on your bad financial decisions, you may find yourself repeating them, because that is your focus.

It is important to keep yourself focused on ways to improve your financial decisions and keep them in line with your financial plan. Yes, you might regret a decision, but make the conscious choice not to dwell on it. Instead, learn from it and move forward. Life, especially when it comes to finances, is a series of learning experiences. The better you are at accepting the lessons, the better decisions you will be able to make in the future. I find inspiration and humor in the lyrics of one of my favorite songs by Chumbawamba, "I get knocked down, but I get up again, you're never gonna keep me down."

Now that you have that mindset (and that song stuck in your head), you can keep yourself from making financial decisions based on your sunk costs and focus on maximizing your earnings. That starts by focusing on finding the right investments for you. With that in mind, let's talk about the Rule of 72.

3) QUICK INTEREST CALCULATIONS USING THE RULE OF 72

One of your biggest concerns about an investment should be, "What am I going to get out of this?" While you wouldn't want to ask that of a date, it's perfectly acceptable, in fact it's expected, to ask that of a potential investment. All of us want a way to determine the upside of a financial opportunity. Now there are several ways to analyze a financial investment, but it often comes down to how long it will take for an investment to pay off. Want to double your holdings? The Rule of 72 can tell you how long it will take, based on the specific interest rate. Just divide 72 by the interest rate to learn how long it will take to double your initial investment.

For example, if you are looking at an investment with an interest rate of 6 percent, then 72 divided by 6 gets you 12 years. You can then take that information and use it to determine if that timeframe will work with your overall financial plan. Granted, you may find that other factors will play a part in determining your return as well, but it is important to have an idea of what you can expect before you put money into an investment.

This is a rough estimate, of course, but it's pretty effective. Recognize that you might find that a return is going to take significantly longer to make you money. So even if you find it an interesting opportunity, you may opt to not invest in order to take advantage of a different opportunity that will give you a faster return on your money.

In fact, you can also turn the equation around to determine the interest rate you are looking at if someone promises to double your returns in a set amount of time. Twice as much money in 12 years? Divide 72 by 12 and you get an interest rate of 6 percent. This rule lets you evaluate investment opportunities quickly and decide where to put your money in a way that will help you to grow your investments to meet long-term financial goals.

Keep in mind, future earnings are not something that you can count on, so how you use the dollars that you have now are going to have greater weight than potential earnings. You know that old saying, "Don't count your chickens before the eggs hatch."

4) THE TIME VALUE OF MONEY

According to this concept, a dollar you receive today is worth more than a dollar you will get tomorrow. You will have opportunity to invest that dollar immediately and begin earning more revenue from it (and also avoid losing value because of inflation).

It is important to recognize that money from your investments needs to be put to work. Don't be quick to spend it. Making frivolous or useless purchases means you are making a choice to spend on meaningless things and activities and in doing so, you are draining your ability to invest and grow. Focus on how you can essentially create a chain of investments, all working to grow an income stream for you to use in retirement or even for a big purchase that is part of your financial plan (think a house or car). Growth is a long-term process and it is imperative that you do make the time for it.

When you are waiting for an investment to pay off, then you are waiting for your money to work for you. One of the ways that you can save money is by limiting your interest payments. When you are making money from investments, which is then reinvested, you create an income stream that can allow you to pay cash for items, or put down a larger down payment, thus helping to reduce those interest payments, or eliminate them altogether.

Again, this helps you make certain calls about your purchases -- and your income. It's the old "one bird in the hand is worth two in a bush" theory in action for your wallet.

These four concepts have served me well over the years. Now let's focus in on the five steps that will help you to remain financially sound as you invest and grow your income to meet your financial goals.

WHY MONEY MATTERS

Before I talk about the steps, I want you to understand that money has a place and purpose in your life. Whatever adventures or experiences you want to have, you are going to need money to do it. That money is also going to be a key part of fulfilling your life's purpose, simply because money is a resource that can help you get things done. Regardless of if your goal in life is to have a non-profit that helps others or to create a company to bring a product or process to market, the truth is that money will be a resource that you need.

Since you and I can agree on that, let's start talking about your financial goals by first talking about your life goals.

STEP 1 - BUDGETING: YOUR PERSONAL BUSINESS PLAN

You have goals you want to accomplish, experience, and create in this life. This is simply a reality we all share. By defining your goals, you are able to determine what financial moves are necessary to achieve them. Too often, personal goals are overlooked or under-appreciated when creating a financial plan. Your personal goals and your financial plan need to be in sync for you to be successful at achieving either one.

For instance, if you know that your financial plan is going to allow you to achieve your personal goals, then it will help you maintain the excitement and vision you have for your life. This knowledge will help keep up the momentum during tough times or difficult circumstances when you are making sacrifices.

Budgeting should be the first part of your financial plan, because it will show the money you have coming in and going out. Once you understand your cash flow, then you have all the information you need to make a sound financial plan. Your budget will allow you to make good choices about how you want to use your money and where you can make changes in your spending habits to align your personal goals with your financial goals.

As part of that budgeting process, you need to look at the choices you make on a daily basis. Consider that if you take out that Tinder date on Saturday night maybe you can't afford to play golf on Sunday. If you really want to golf, then maybe you have to Netflix and chill with $1 bottles of beer or a $7 bottle of wine and takeout pizza instead of your dinner and a movie date. We all have to make choices. Just make sure your choices are good choices. You may find that you are sabotaging yourself by the financial decisions you make every day.

The good news is that you don't have to try to figure out a budget on your own or hire a professional to do it for you. All you need is that device that sometimes acts as another appendage – your cell phone. Yes, there is another reason that your cell phone is your best friend because there's an app for that (for budgeting, that is). Actually, there are several apps for that, you just have to choose the one that works best for you.

I use Mint to track my personal bank accounts, credit cards, investments and bills – it creates a budget based on my income and expenses and reminds me when I have a payment due date. I love that my whole financial life is accessible in one place and that I can monitor activity at a glance. One of my daughters uses Clarity Money, which has similar features plus the added benefit of helping to cancel unwanted subscriptions. With an app, you won't have to wonder if you are spending too much money shopping or eating out, you can see it in full color. Knowledge is power, and this knowledge can be used to change your spending behavior to match your financial goals.

For instance, think about that $5 cup of coffee you stop to buy every morning to start your day. That money falls into the sunk costs pot, because you are not getting that money back and it is not working for you. Imagine how much money you could save if you took that $5 per day for a year and saved or invested it – you would have more than $1,825. Going back to those two daughters of mine, one likes to buy and play internet games, a lot – can you guess which one? I'll tell you it's not the one that uses Clarity Money. If you are having trouble saving to meet your long-term goals, then it might be worth exploring using an app to help you get control of your spending.

It is not about giving up your lifestyle, but making your lifestyle adhere to your financial priorities, instead of letting your lifestyle dictate your priorities. Everyone has time to know their money.

Part of achieving any financial goal is to create a nest egg of funds to work with, which serves as a basis for your investment portfolio. Using your budget, you can designate a specific percentage to go into your savings.

STEP 2 – SAVING

The point of saving is to create a financial resource that you can use to build your income streams. These income streams can be diversified, but the point is that saving has to be a priority in order to improve your financial situation and allow you to reach your goals. Here are just a few reasons why saving is important.

1. You have a nest egg for emergencies. Time and time again, financial emergencies have sunk individuals who appear to be doing well, simply because they had nothing to fall back on. Once it happens, they have a financial issue, one that can have a ripple effect across other areas of their lives. Point blank, having an emergency, such as an unexpected car repair or house repair, should not financially sink you. Experts recommend that your savings for emergency needs to cover six months of your living expenses. Once you reach that goal, keep saving a set amount to grow your emergency fund. If you have to use some of it for an emergency, then replace it as soon as possible.

2. You can save for larger purchases. You know that paying cash for items can save you money in the long run, because you won't pay interest on top of the purchase cost. When you designate savings for specific

purchases, it allows you to reach your financial goals without acquiring payments. Plus, once you make that big purchase, you can start saving for the next big item or event.

3. You can save to invest to build income streams. Once you have achieved your emergency savings goal, start building a savings that is specifically for investments. These funds should not be used for any other purpose, allowing you to adjust the rate of return to meet your goals.

Clearly, saving is important because it gives you a stepping stone to meet your financial needs and personal dreams. Now, I want to transition to the exploring the possibilities that you can create with a savings that was started for investing.

STEP 3 – INVESTING

When you reach the point that you have started an investment savings account, you have plenty of opportunities. From stocks and bonds to direct investing in a business, you have multiple ways to grow your investment dollars. That being said, it is important to choose investments that fall in line with your goals and your risk tolerance level.

For instance, if you are at the beginning of your career, you might find yourself more inclined to look for high return, risky investments. Why? Many of those who are younger see time on their side and recognize that they have time to recover from a loss. Alternately, as you reach specific benchmarks or get closer to achieving your financial goals, you will start to make less risky investments.

Another potential scenario is that you are planning to get married or start a family, in which case, you might be more concerned with the risk of losing the primary financial provider. In a case like this, you may be more interested in investing in a disability or life insurance policy or even starting a college fund. After all, not all investments are created equal.

Where you are in your life can play a large part in what type of investments you choose to take on. Additionally, you might take on investments that are less time-consuming because they give you the ability to do more of what you enjoy. On the other hand, you might want to be more hands-on in your investments, so that may be a factor in the types of investments you choose.

Your investment plan should be personalized to you and designed to meet your needs. I want you to recognize that working with a financial advisor can help you to determine the best investments for you.

Many of the individuals I work with even consider investing in themselves, which means starting their own business. If you want to explore your entrepreneurial spirit, that can be a great way to invest and see your returns grow, using your investment dollars and sweat equity. Again, I encourage you to put any investment up against your financial plan. Ask yourself the hard questions about whether it will work towards accomplishing your goals. Doing so is critical to keeping you focused and on the path to achieving both your financial and personal goals. Just keep in mind that it takes time to grow and any time frames set by you can be changed, especially if the situation changes.

STEP 4 – AVOIDING MOST KINDS OF DEBT

Debt can drown you financially and make it difficult for you to achieve your financial goals. When you look at your budget, do you see areas where you are spending money on payments regularly? That is money which is not being used to create income streams or to reach your financial goals.

Be picky when you are choosing to take on debt. I recommend that you only finance things that will bring in money or pay for themselves. It's okay to finance your education because you expect your education to yield you a higher paying career. Do not finance your vacation because you will have nothing but memories to show for it. You can pay for your business advertising with a credit card but not your groceries. Avoid running up your credit cards, leaving yourself strapped with payments. The interest payments can quickly exceed your budget and be a drain. Use the cash in your bank account to pay for your living expenses because the interest on credit cards is usually greater than the interest you earn on money deposited in the bank.

Some debt can be beneficial and preferable because it shares the risk. I am talking about debt that involves investing. For instance, if you are building a real estate portfolio of rentals and you have $100,000 to invest, you might find that you choose to split that $100,000 into down payments for five properties instead of just buying one for $100,000. The reason is that you can increase your cash flow across five properties and they can also cover their own overhead. In the meantime, you are creating equity that you can tap into later to purchase more properties. The point is that you want to use your investment cash to maximize your income opportunities. Do not limit yourself because you want to avoid all debt – some debt can be good.

When weighing your debt options, be sure to look at interest rates. Do not feel as if you are limited to one lender or one financing option. Shop around and make sure that you get the lowest possible rate for your debt with the best payment plan to meet your investment needs. Also, make sure that any investment purchased with debt is going to have a positive cash flow. Some investments may not have a positive cash flow initially but will overtime as the debt is paid down. For other investments, it is the value which grows over time that offsets the lack of a positive cash flow.

Again, it is important to work with a professional who can help you determine what types of debt you want to take on regarding your investments and what debt you want to avoid.

In the end, this step is mostly focused on helping you to avoid debt that drains you financially, without giving you any type of return. Think about the cost of those daily coffees. The focus of this step needs to be on defining the lifestyle you want and then investing in order to be able to afford it. If you opt to live a lifestyle that drains your investments, you could be shortchanging yourself for the future, thus limiting your ability to reach your dreams.

STEP 5 – EVALUATE AND ASSESS: ONGOING PROCESS

I call this step, "the shit happens" part of your plan. Yes, it would be nice if life happened exactly as we planned it, but real life is no fairy tale. The reality is that you made a plan based on the life you wanted to live and all the messy stuff that got in your way is why you had contingency plans, emergency funds and cushions built into your plan. Shit happens, and you deal. You deal by adapting to your new situation. Update your plan as if it is a living, breathing organism.

For instance, you had an accident that kept you from working for six months. That would be both physically and financially draining. This is only a temporary setback. Now you need to reset your goals to achieve your plans, because you may need to focus on rebuilding instead of growth. Still, the point is to make adjustments that help you achieve your goals, thus not allowing the circumstances to overwhelm you and derail your finances permanently.

This need to make adjustments also applies to your investments. I recommend at least once per quarter that you review your investments to make sure they are performing as expected. You don't want to waste your resources on underperforming investments.

Are there areas you might want to expand even further, or do you need to eliminate some investments because they no longer fit your financial goals? Doing these reviews regularly can help you to keep your financial life on track with your personal life. When the two are in sync, then you will find that your life continues to improve. This harmony makes it possible to achieve what you want, no matter the setbacks you might occasionally encounter.

Keep in mind that evaluating and assessing will always be ongoing processes. The fluidity of life is that you can create plans, but events may alter those plans or even offer you new opportunities and experiences that you might not have even considered.

It is important to keep your mind open, both to new investments and to new experiences and opportunities in your personal life. They often can dovetail together more than you ever realize.

Financially, your world is built on the decisions that you make throughout your life. Always know the direction you want to go before you start your journey. When you make decisions without direction, your life will be like a boat without a rudder. It goes all over but doesn't actually get anywhere. The waves take the boat in multiple directions without a clear destination.

I want you to define your path and then work in harmony with that by making choices to complement it. Even with a defined path, it can be easy to make decisions that run contrary to your goals, as I discussed earlier in this chapter. When I work with individuals, I help them to not only define their path, but also to determine the types of goals that align with their paths. Then, I can help them to find the right investments and set financial goals to help them go further on that path.

Growth happens by learning from those people who inspire you to do and be more. We all have time to learn and grow.

Please email Ursula Garrett at ugarrett@cpagarrett.com or visit her website www.cpagarrett.com

Break Through Your Barriers & Live Your Dreams

SANDRA WESTLAND

Every woman deserves to feel powerful and successful, and the opportunity to do so stands right before her. She doesn't have to be a warrior to smite every dragon or burn down every obstacle that stands in her way. She simply needs to connect with and be her real, authentic self. So her journey to success begins by standing still, by being curious about the world of potential that exists within her and in front of her, and by understanding her inner world in order to ignite change in her outer one towards her success.

But, what stops her from becoming the author of her own life, from being all she can be? The glass ceiling, the unofficial barrier that prevents women from rising up to executive positions or from running their successful businesses, does still exist. Yet, in my twenty-five years of education, hypno-psychotherapy and peak performance training, I see, more significantly, an individual's own inner glass ceiling capping and limiting the success in life that is there for the taking.

To be a woman is to be extraordinary. We all have it within us to move beyond an ordinary life and its everyday limitations to embrace our desires and possibilities, harness our untold natural potential and live the life we are meant to live —a life of personal freedom in which we simply are our natural, awesome selves. Your power is switched on when you embrace, embody, express and enjoy being a woman. Your energy is released when you learn to live truly in your own skin. I love being a woman, and I love continuing to find out just what that is like for me.

This is a journey of discovering your place in life as a woman and as a woman in business, a voyage into your inner mind's processing and the terrain of your inner world, deeper than your conscious mind can be aware of. It is an expedition through self-alignment, forming the detail of your desired outcomes, shaping your life to fit with your passions, sourcing the energy that drives you, thus smashing your glass ceiling and allowing your transformation to unfold. Just as I experienced my own first steps, I want you also to stride out along this path and the journey of becoming your potential. The message I write within the pages of *Smashing Your Glass Ceiling* takes you through this fascinating journey where "Wow, I didn't realize that" and "No wonder I wasn't getting to where I wanted to" are familiar insights.

HOW DOES IT ALL WORK?

The tools you will need for such a journey of self-discovery are drawn from Neuro-Linguistic Programming (NLP), guided imagery, and a gentle questing into uncovering your own uniqueness and meaning in life. In blending these time-tested methods into one programme, it's possible to break through all that's holding you back in life.

From my own personal experience as a woman and as a psychotherapist and trainer, I've found that one of the most powerful tools we naturally have and need to embrace first is the power of imagination; even if you think you have one or not, you really do have an amazing, creative imagination. It just may need awakening and a little encouraging. I would love to show you just how powerful your imagination can be and how crucial it is to connect with you and be your own woman. In beginning this imaginative journey, you are sparking off a chain of events that produce fundamental changes in your physical body, starting with the neurological processes that will link to your biology and produce within you "decision states" leading to the different outcomes that you want, easily and naturally. Imagine the decisions that you can make or the actions that you can take when you are feeling confident, in balance and aligned to your vision, compared to the choices that you opt for when you are upset, anxious, depressed and out of sync with yourself.

By guiding your imagination, you can form an internal vision in which you are taking the right path for you to succeed in your life, and then formulate just what that is. As you immerse yourself in the excitement and the thrill of being on the right road to greatness, you tap into the inner confidence and self-reliance, inner freedom and success awareness that generate your momentum to smashing your glass ceiling. The power is always within you. It's just a case of summoning and connecting with it.

137

Imagine also gaining new understanding into how you process information from your "now" experiences, how you view the world, how you communicate with others and how they communicate with you. Imagine how much easier your life would be. You can learn how to recognize ways of processing external data and how, by modifying your communication in a way that makes sense to others, your relationships become infinitely warmer, richer and more connected.

Think about meeting me in the flesh for the first time, already knowing how my inner world works. Wouldn't it be good to know I'm an auditory person? Why? Well, my world is very much filtered through sounds. I will be finely tuned into noise … all noise. I will get distracted with too much of it, and I will recognize very slight changes in your voice, tone and pitch. So I will hear a hint of doubt or an emotion rising from within you just by hearing your voice. If you speak too slowly or very loudly, this will create a dissonance within me. If you use language that talks about "viewing something" or "seeing what you mean" or "having a handle on this or that" instead of "sounds like" or "listen to", I will feel a mismatch between us. Don't click your pen or tap it on the table if you want me to be relaxed! It's only a slight inner discomfort, but it undeniably shapes how I experience you and your communication. Upon our meeting, if you appreciate my world and I appreciate yours, we will hit it off with ease. I will look to communicate to you through your world, which may be visual, auditory, kinesthetic or auditory digital, all very different ways of experiencing and processing, and you can do the same for me.

GETTING TO KNOW YOUR GLASS CEILING

Your internal glass ceiling may have been created from prejudgments, prejudices, cultural and social attitudes that operate deep within the unconscious, taken in when young. So, it's crucial to find these out and know how they work for you, to understand the inner conflicts that are holding you back and what they mean. In speaking with a senior executive upon her reading *Smashing Your Glass Ceiling*, she'd suddenly become aware of how she was dressing like a man for her banking boardroom meetings. It wasn't her at all, but after further exploration, she realized she had unconsciously thought it would help men relate to her and allow her to be "taken seriously". She was shocked at how unconscious this had been, but she was relieved to learn it and is now enjoying the fun of finding out who she is as a woman in business and what clothes this exploration leads her to wearing. It is only by excavating these unconscious gender biases and other judgments that contribute towards making your own ceiling that you can reveal your real, natural self to yourself and the world. In understanding yourself more and knowing just who you are and how you are in the world, you become free to choose how to respond to situations and to people, and then you really begin to own your own life.

I am wondering just what you are thinking, having read these thousand plus words. Is this possible for you or is your glass ceiling giving you bother, preventing you from imagining and thinking of all that you can be? What does your ceiling hold and what is it whispering to you right now? What is your "default" setting?

Are you someone who assumes you won't find a car parking space and prove yourself right, or do you simply know that it doesn't matter where you park and thus usually find one just when and where you need it? Is a potential redundancy at work a chance to do something different, or a terrible catastrophe that you will never escape? Your attitudes play a massive part in your life experiences, and to how much you can grow. Zig Ziglar's famous saying "Your attitude determines your altitude" is so true. So, how do your attitudes determine how successful you can be?

I have lived and refined through my own personal journey a framework of all the things that are crucial to help you aspire to be. Let's make a start right now, something to get you thinking. Let's peek into those achieving just what you want and begin to emulate some of what they do and how they are. It's as good a place as any to start!

In NLP terms, this is called "modeling". In modeling the behaviors and habits of successful people, we're seeking to learn from successful businesswomen and successful women just what it is that they do, and what it is that they have that makes them successful; not to become them, but to incorporate their winning behaviours into our repertoire, choosing those which are congruent with us and amplifying them. I often explore other women that I admire and am drawn to. In carefully watching what they do and exploring this within my own life, in my way, I can open up to further resources that I naturally have, but have yet to connect with. In Sue Knight's' words, "If you spot it, you've got it." (NLP at Work, 2013)

Now to stoke up those neurological pathways as we vamp it up a little more and transport you forward into your own fabulous future. Familiarize yourself with the state of being successful with no glass ceiling, as if you've already accomplished that level of success, a dress rehearsal if you like. Put on the mantle of success and ask yourself how and what do you feel, how would your day evolve, what can you do now that you couldn't do before. How would others perceive you? Get your brain to make it a done deal so that it can look for it, search it out and create it. This is the self-fulfilling prophecy at its most positive, potent and powerful.

Anticipate now becoming friendly and familiar with a future you who has everything you need and want and to be able to use the guidance of that future you – the answers may very well surprise you. My future self enlightened me as to my fear of success! This helped me find my inner glass ceiling and the meaning of it all, so I could smash it and really begin to find out just what I could do and what was possible in life. I believe that to guide others you have to have lived the journey yourself, and so my own personal journey has and is this path too, encompassing where I am finding myself ... as a woman, an educator, therapist and businesswoman. This is a journey I don't ever intend to stop.

PEELING BACK THE ONION

There is so much more to explore! As humans, we've infinite depths, so exploring your inner beliefs, your values and mission is crucial for success. It's the peeling back of the onion, layer by layer (corny, I know), but I assure you that the exploration, while deep, is richly rewarding. Wouldn't you rather know what's holding you back and why you may feel frustrated with yourself? I know I would. I simply want to make the most of my time on this earth and experience it as much as possible. Life is to be lived and not simply endured and got through.

Excavate your inner beliefs, isolate the limiting ones that have held you back, and then you will easily and naturally begin to fly! Once figured out, you become empowered as you re-think and re-frame beliefs into being resourceful, productive and desirable, and turn them into second nature.

Let's go one deeper. Do you know just what it is that you value, all those things that are really important to you? Are they aligned with your life? These are your GPS, and if you're frustrated, feel trapped in the mundane of life or have unwanted physical/emotional symptoms, then value fine-tuning is needed for you to move forward in the direction that you want to go. Let's not be sidetracked by detours, road closures and an unclear destination. Being authentic and all that you need to know is what you value so that you're able to craft your mission for the ultimate alignment. In *Smashing Your Glass Ceiling* or my Success workshops , you will not short-change yourself here. I will journey with you, helping you along the way through a process of simple, yet profoundly powerful steps.

When you are fully aligned, there will be no holding you back. You'll meet the right person at the right time, and you'll have the right skills to achieve your goals. Everything will fall into place like a jigsaw puzzle, and you'll have "the strength, the patience, and the passion to reach for the stars", to borrow the words of a courageously inspiring woman, Harriet Tubman.

LOADING UP ON INTERNAL RESOURCES

It's not all plain sailing, and you *will* be derailed by the unexpected, but what makes someone a success is their ability to keep going, even when challenged. So, one of the final steps in the Programme is to load you up with the internal resources to get you through when things get sticky, and when, quite frankly, you wonder why you bother. NLP strategies reprogram how we react and respond to such times, making a monumental difference to how you experience your life. If you're feeling down on yourself, I will show you that you can change your physiology. If you're getting increasingly anxious about an upcoming meeting, you can change your self-talk, the inner conversation you're having with yourself, to something more upbeat, more encouraging and more positive.

Powerful NLP strategies are there for you to use at any time and in any situation. Your life will be richer and filled with more options when you are able to redirect your thinking and focus, stay resourceful in stressful situations, and generate behaviors and outcomes that are positive for you and your life.

Finally, if this chapter has inspired you to delve deeper into Smashing your Glass Ceiling, the book comes with a number of bonuses, some of which can be downloaded from my website, www.SmashingYourGlassCeiling.com for you to enjoy absolutely free. So, get started now and embrace the fact that you are an extraordinary woman.

TAKING THE FIRST STEP

All of us have to start somewhere. I did when I was thirty-four, when I found myself looking at twenty-six more years before retirement, counting the years and the days till the next school holiday. Not how I imagined my life would be.

By becoming curious, asking questions of myself and tapping into effective life-changing techniques that opened me up to the power and potential of the mind, I'm on a fascinating journey. I'm continuing to smash my own internal glass ceiling, and am living out my passion to enhance the lives of other women. I am certainly not "sorted out", nor have I "self-actualized" and not every day is "grrreat", but I know that every day is an adventure with the chance to grow further and find out more about just what is possible.

The more women I meet and work with, the more I learn and the more I gather evidence to support my belief that, as women, we owe it to ourselves to be extraordinary. This is my invitation to you to take the first steps with me on your own journey of becoming all you wish to be.

Sandra Westland is an experienced educator, therapist and successful businesswoman who helps others to find their passion and fulfil their dreams. She has a Master's degree in Existential Psychotherapy, an Education Honours degree, and is a practicing Advanced Hypnotherapist and NLP practitioner. Her doctoral thesis explores women and their relationship with their bodies. She is the author of Smash Your Glass Ceiling and co-author of Thinking Therapeutically.

Sandra is a Director of the Contemporary College of Therapeutic Studies, where she trains people at life changing junctures to be aspiring therapists, so they too can enjoy the enriching privilege of helping others to find their path in life. She is also a co-founder of Self Help School™, which provides psycho-education for the public and is an international speaker on the power of the mind for change.

Enter Into a Passionate Relationship with Your Own Life

SILVANA AVRAM

Have you ever wondered whether there is more to life than meets the eye? Do you feel that despite all your achievements true fulfilment still eludes you?

Join me on this transformational journey where you will learn to see yourself and your life in a different light.

- You will find out how to ask the right questions.

- You will learn to identify the main reason why you find yourself trapped in the same vicious circle.

- You will redefine the true meaning of being and uncover the source of deep fulfilment.

- You will be able to decide whether you are ready to embark on the journey to personal fulfilment.

My passionate plea to you is to allow this introduction to the secret of lasting fulfilment to work as a powerful catalyst for you. Should you want to explore the topics addressed here in more depth I invite you to read my book "Being You And Loving You – The Ultimate Guide To Fulfilment" – where I guide you through twelve life changing steps to true fulfilment. Together with the book you will also find plenty of free materials, insights and support at www.BeingYouAndLovingYou.com

It is the aim of this chapter to empower you to start your journey to true fulfilment. Are you ready? Let's dive in!

YOUR JOURNEY TO FULFILMENT STARTS WITH ASKING THE RIGHT QUESTIONS

"The Universe contains three things that cannot be destroyed;
Being, Awareness and LOVE"

— *Deepak Chopra*

"What is the meaning of life?" Human beings have searched for an answer to this question for millennia. Sages, philosophers, religious figures and scientists have all put forward their hypotheses, and each interpretation added yet another nuance to a mystery that remains as fascinating and as alluring as it has always been.

So: "Why are we here?" And why is it that this most important question of all is also one of the most avoided? Perhaps we have long accepted that there is no answer to it. Perhaps facing this question feels so…unsettling that we prefer to bury it under more…urgent matters. Like finding a job and paying the next bill.

I put to you another possibility. I believe that "Why are we here?" is indeed an unanswerable question. At least for the time being. And so is *"What is the meaning of life?"*

Why? Because they are too vast…and too vague!

Does that mean I am advising you to drop the questioning altogether and simply get on with your life? No, not at all! Not if you want to live a joyous, meaningful life. Not if you are looking for true fulfilment. In fact, if this is what you are after, it is vitally important to keep questioning.

But you must learn to ask the right questions.

I believe that each one of us must start with the more manageable "Why *am I* here?" or "What is the meaning of *my* life?"

I believe that each one of us must take responsibility for our own answers.

You see, when you allow someone else to answer these questions for you, you give away your power (and with that your responsibility). You may like a particular answer/ philosophy for a while and you may find it resonates with you – you may even dedicate your life to promoting it – but it will still not be yours – and as such it will not fully transform your life, it will not bring you the fulfilment you crave. You may read as many books as you want and you may attend endless wonderful seminars…They will all help you feel good for a while and you are sure to get some valuable insight. But no person and no book can truly change your life for you. Only when you find the strength and the courage to stay with the question of meaning long enough to allow for your own answer to be born in you, will you find the infinite joy and freedom that come from knowing. It is only *your own* answer that will truly transform *your life*. It is owning that answer that brings true fulfilment.

If your life is a riddle, the only way to fully - fill it… is to find your own answer to it.

Now that you know where to start…how do you actually do it?

You can find your own answer by asking the right questions, either on your own or by engaging in a philosophical dialogue with friends and other people interested in the same quest for meaning. You must be patient and tenacious, and not give up at the first signs of exhaustion or disappointment. After all, the question of meaning is the most challenging question of all, and many choose to avoid it altogether. But if you stay with it, if you make it an intrinsic part of your journey, sooner or later you will be rewarded.

You will not be alone in your endeavour. One of the most famous of the Delphic maxims inscribed in the pronaos (forecourt) of the Temple of Apollo at Delphi, Ancient Greece, and quoted by many, most famously by Socrates as the main character in Plato's dialogues, was *"Know Thyself"*. Through the ages there have been many who have embarked on this arduous journey.

Today, there is a modern variant of the life-transforming dialogues left to posterity by Plato: the coaching dialogue. The Philosopher is replaced by the more modest Coach. They are similar, however, in that the Coach, like the Greek philosopher but unlike a religious figure or a mentor, is not providing the answers. Instead, she or he is merely providing you with the right questions, gently challenging you when you go off track and often holding a symbolic mirror in which you start to see your true reflection and find your own answers.

It is a true measure of our 21st Century's *Age of Knowledge* that Coaching has become such an accessible experience. Perhaps this is a sign that more and more amongst us are ready and willing to stay with the question of meaning and find the true purpose of our lives. Perhaps more and more people are ready to embark on the journey to true fulfilment. Are you?

BEING SUCCESSFUL IS NOT THE SAME AS SUCCEEDING AT BEING

"What makes you think human beings are sentient and aware? There's no evidence for it. Human beings never think for themselves, they find it too uncomfortable. For the most part, members of our species simply repeat what they are told – and become upset if they are exposed to any different view. The characteristic human trait is not awareness but conformity.."

— *Michael Crichton*

"I am a human being, not a human doing. Don't equate your self-worth with how well you do things in life. You aren't what you do. If you are what you do, then when you don't...you aren't."

— *Dr. Wayne Dyer*

Before we proceed to consider what your journey to true fulfilment might look like when you embark on a path of enquiry and examination, I would like you to briefly stop and take a look at your life right now.

Do you love your life? Do you love yourself? Do you feel deep gratitude and awe about who you are? Do you feel blissful, fulfilled and radiant, sharing your wisdom and your light with everyone else, in compassion?

Chances are that you don't.

Chances are that you don't even believe this is possible!!

But if it were possible, would you like to feel like this? Would you like to live your life with absolute joy, and share your happiness with others?

I hope your answer to that last question is yes.

If it is, you have already taken the first step to fulfilment.

You see, most people have already given up on personal fulfilment. Most people have somehow fallen into the trap of believing that there is nothing more to life than work, duty, supporting family and friends, and the occasional recreation. It may sound incredible, but most people have convinced themselves that life is more about sacrifice and suffering than about being happy. If asked, of course everyone would say they want to be happy. Yet most people spend their lives doing things that take them farther and farther away from being joyful and fulfilled.

Most people spend most of their lives *doing* things. In fact doing so many things that they don't have the time to stop and ask *why* they are doing them.

Most people spend their lives doing so many things that they forget to Be.

But how can I forget to be? I hear you ask.

What else is there to 'being' that I haven't got already? Is it not enough that I am…alive? How can I be …being? How can I Be more?

You see…rocks and trees and animals are too. They exist. Life flows through them and expresses through them without encountering much opposition. They are pure expressions of life.

And so are we. Except for the fact that we also have the wonderful gifts of thought, of mind…of consciousness.

I want you to consider that maybe, just maybe, for us humans it is not enough to be alive, to truly Be. If it were, we would all be happy – or at least at ease. We would not ask questions. We would not search for more.

What makes us different is that we have the gift of being able to be aware of being. It is this gift, and whether or not we choose to use it, that makes all the difference.

In order to truly Be as a human being you must be aware of who you are – of your potential. You must get involved in "being", become responsible for your "being", become the co-creator of your life.

When, on the other hand, we choose not to use the gift of awareness, we spend most of our lives doing things, being alive without truly being aware of the mystery, the complexity and the beauty of our being. We allow doing to take over, we throw ourselves into doing with a vengeance, seeking solace in temporary achievements that often leave us emptier than before.

Why and how does this happen? When we live without fully being present to our own lives, to our own being, we function on automatic pilot much of the time. Most of the functions we perform require so little of our conscious input that we get used to being disengaged. It's easier. We do the minimum and we get by. If we are "lucky" we can spend our whole life without having to account for the huge lack of ... presence in it. For the most part, everyone is doing the same, and we are covered. No one will know. No one will dare ask.

But is that truly "lucky"? Is our life really about "getting by"?

If it were, mere survival would qualify as fulfilment. You would already and at all times feel fulfilled. Yet most of us know deep down inside our hearts that our lives must be more than just survival.

Perhaps our life is about success?

The difference between success and fulfilment is that success, as it tends to be defined, is still at the level of doing. You can become successful by following instructions and still staying on autopilot. In fact, the more autopilot-friendly the system you follow, the more successful you probably are in that particular area.

It is a common mistake to equate success with fulfilment. Many people who do, realize that success has not brought them the fulfilment they wished for. Many of these people spend years wondering where they went wrong and what's missing.

Our society seems to conspire to push us towards a narrowly defined form of success that rarely allows any space for true fulfilment. In other words, our misinterpretations are not entirely our fault. We are taught from early on to play by the (widely accepted) rules. We trust our parents and our teachers, and we unwittingly follow in their footsteps. We keep ourselves busy doing so many things that we have little time for self-exploration or personal inquiry, for Being. It is this restless drive for doing more and more that slowly but surely derails us from the only achievement that matters: understanding, accepting and expressing – in fact Being - our true self. Unless we stop to ask the right questions we don't even realise what we are missing.

To sum it up, success in doing cannot lead to fulfilment, for the simple reason that it involves operating at a different level.

To achieve true fulfilment you must operate at the level of Being.

It is not being successful at doing that will make you feel fulfilled.

To be fulfilled you must succeed at Being.

* * * *

So far we have learnt that in order to be fulfilled you must start by asking the right questions: "What is the meaning of my life?" "Why am I here?"

Tackling these and similar questions of meaning helps you become aware: aware that there is more to life than meets the eye; aware that as a human being it is not enough to be alive…Nor is it enough to be doing many things.

We then looked at what happens when you don't ask these questions. When you avoid questioning the true meaning of your life you get sucked into a life of endless doing with very little time for Being – and hence, with very little or no chance of feeling fulfilled.

For most people the question of meaning is an intimidating one, and one they'd rather put aside. After all, why take responsibility for one's life when it seems easier to just get by? Many people "succeed" in avoiding this question altogether. They also miss the opportunity of living deeply fulfilling, joyful lives. For others, something happens that forces them to wake up to it. It could be an unexpected turn of fate, a tragic event, even a major bonus, like winning the lottery, that pushes them to take a deeper look in the mirror. At those times they discover that there is a whole new dimension to 'being' that they were completely ignoring before. It is then up to them to embark on a journey of discovery that should ultimately lead them to true fulfilment.

There is, of course, a more natural, organic way that comes when you simply decide to take responsibility for your life and actively explore the gifts it promises to offer. You do it because you realize this is the only way you are going to feel truly happy and fulfilled. You do it because you want to be a co–creator in your life and express your full potential.

Along the way you may need the help of a friend, a sage or a coach – and you may be able to help others – but ultimately each one of us must find our own answers in order to express the true richness of our lives.

Once you are on the path to fulfilment there is no going back. You taste the ecstasy of being alive. Everything thereafter is a miraculous discovery, a wonderful adventure, a self-affirming deed and a deeply fulfilling expression of who you are. You have been kissed by life.

TRUE FULFILMENT COMES FROM AN AUTHENTIC AND LOVING RELATIONSHIP WITH YOUR LIFE

"The first step toward change is awareness. The second step is acceptance."

— *Nathaniel Branden*

We have established that in order to find true fulfilment you must be able to start with the right question and you must be able and willing to stay with it until you find your own answer. This is no easy journey. But it is the only one that will get you to true fulfilment. And as such, it is the most exciting journey of all.

If you are looking for deeper fulfilment, if you have started to realise that fulfilment will not come from doing more "stuff", chances are that you are already awakening to the possibility of an infinitely richer you. It does not matter how long it took you to get to this point. What matters is that you are ready: ready to embark on the beautiful, empowering, liberating and ultimately fulfilling journey of Being; ready to Be. Now.

Congratulations! Let the journey begin!

* * * *

As a coach, I can never get tired of seeing my clients find true joy and meaning in their lives. It often feels as if I watch them learn how to fly. And when they take off on their own…The sense of unlimited potential, freedom and happiness that comes with finding your own answer to the mystery of life is truly indescribable. One must experience it to be able to understand it.

But, if you will allow me, I would like to share with you what you might expect along the way.

There are two essential ingredients that will ensure a successful journey.

1.   In order to be fulfilled you must first learn to Be.

2.   Then you must learn how to Love Being.

As we touched upon earlier, truly Being requires presence and awareness.

True fulfilment comes when you and your life become one. When you live passionately…fully. To be one with life you must first wake up to Being; you must be aware of who you really are.

To start with, this will involve exploring your strengths, your talents, your gifts. It will mean looking at what makes you *you*, what makes you unique. In case you are already backing off in fear, rest assured. Every one of us is unique. Your special features, your memories and stories, your thoughts and feelings, your desires and dreams…all these make you a world unto itself, a uniquely beautiful expression of life, an exquisite original work of art in constant motion. There is no one else in the entire universe like you. There has never been and there will never be! You just have to muster the courage to embrace this truth! And allow it to transform you! It will help to have someone else hold the mirror, but once you learn to look at yourself in this way you will be able to see your life in a different light.

(To learn more about how you can embrace and celebrate your uniqueness visit www.SilvanaAvram.com)

It will then be important to find ways to truly express who you are; to listen to your heart and let it teach you everything you had tried to forget. Becoming aware of your thought patterns and connecting with your deepest emotions will enable you to re-define yourself. Then you can move one step further and try your hand at re-creating who you are. Being you is the gift you were given. Accepting this gift and then bettering it will be the gift you give back to life. How wonderful. This is pure creation. It's a miraculous process. Let it be fun!

At this point you should be ready to start thinking of how you could share your gift with others. This will become your purpose. That's when the real magic begins. And with it, true joy.

This is the point on your journey when your love relationship with life truly begins. The intimate loving relationship that you have managed to build with yourself expands into a passionate love affair with your life.

Now that you have become the co-creator of your life you must allow yourself to fall in love with your creation. You and your life must become one. This means moving from living your life into allowing your life to live, to express through you. You must be in awe of your life, you must respect it and cherish it and place it above anything else. Because your life is your gift to yourself and to the world. Because your life is the most intimate expression of who you are.

Loving your life is acknowledging and loving the infinite potential that you are. Loving your life with passion will teach you how to love every life with passion – will help you connect with every other life in compassion and joy. Knowing that you have expressed the best of you gives you the licence to feel free, to feel happy, to feel fulfilled.

When you live your life with this intensity there is a point where you will have to lose yourself to find yourself. That is when you must confront your deepest fear. Just as you have learnt to love yourself you must prepare to lose yourself. This is your ultimate act of sacrifice. You understand that your life does not belong to you. And this makes you love it even more. Now living your best possible life truly becomes your mission – and the only measurement of feeling true fulfilment.

You are now close, very close in fact, to fulfilment. You have already had glimpses of it – and you have started to feel its presence more and more poignantly. It is a mysterious, evasive feeling but one that is constant, and constantly making you blush. It permeates your life like a subtle perfume, like the light filling a room – like the presence of joy.

Your wonderful ability to be has now become a living example for others to see. By being you and fulfilling your mission you gift the world with your presence, and your life is the very proof of your fulfilment.

You inspire, you touch other lives and you share your wisdom and your joyful awareness with ease.

You live your life with the profound and blissful awareness of having achieved true fulfilment and the immense gratitude of having been able to do so.

* * * *

How does that feel? I hope you were able to get a glimpse of what it might mean to walk the journey to fulfilment. Often the transformation that takes place is difficult to put into words.

Suffice it to say that in this magical process you and your life will be completely transformed.

You enter a true partnership with life. You fall in love with your life and you become a co-creator of your life. That is the true meaning of being one with life. You live passionately – vibrantly. You express through your life and your life expresses through you.

To love being, to be in love with your life, is to step beyond being you into the miraculous field of living your life in service to Life – of giving your life as a gift back to Life. Everything you do at this level enriches you and enhances your life while affirming Life itself.

True fulfilment comes from being authentic and accomplishing your potential – thus fulfilling and honouring the unique opportunity that your life is.

(Explore more and get inspired with the wealth of insights and materials on the topic of being you, loving you and transcending you…that you will find at: www.BeingYouAndLovingYou.com)

LIVING A FULFILLING LIFE: IF NOT NOW, WHEN?

"Waking up is not a selfish pursuit of happiness, it is a revolutionary stance, from the inside out, for the benefit of all beings in existence."

– Noah Levine

We have explored together what it takes to embark on the journey to personal fulfilment.

We saw that it all starts with asking the right questions. We looked at what might happen when we fail to ask these questions. Then we had a glimpse at what to expect once we embark on this journey. I suppose the only question left is…Are you in?

You see… You either are or you aren't feeling fulfilled right now. And if you aren't, you are faced with a serious choice. True personal fulfilment involves presence and passion. You can't tell your life "I will live you tomorrow" or "I will love you tomorrow." You can't tell your mission, your purpose "I will be with you later." You have to be ready, open to it now. You have to commit to living your best possible life now.

The journey to fulfilment is not the easiest. It does require courage, honesty, a deep sense of wonder, the desire to overcome fears and the capacity to accept life's ephemeral and mysterious nature – and love it all the more for it.

To truly know fulfilment you must make the transition from living at the doing level to living at the Being level. Being successful has nothing to do with being fulfilled. Succeeding at Being has everything to do with it.

To truly succeed at Being you must go on a journey of self-discovery, and learn to celebrate your uniqueness, your richness, your unique expression, your feelings. You must learn to become a conscious co-creator of your life and then find the best ways to share your creation.

With this you move towards learning to love yourself and falling in love with your life. Once you learn to love yourself you must overcome your fear of losing yourself. This gives you the freedom to share yourself with the world.

By doing this you become an inspiration to others. You share the light of awareness with others. Finally you give back your life to Life with and for others – and in this you find ultimate fulfilment.

I don't know of a more wondrous journey – or one that is more worth it. You have been invited. The door has been opened for you. But only you can walk this journey and make your life the most extraordinary adventure of all. It is your life. Will you make it your fulfilment?

FINAL THOUGHT

If these pages have inspired you, you are probably ready to embark on the journey to fulfilment. Sometimes all we need is for someone to point the way. At other times we need someone to hold our hand as we learn how to fly on our own. I believe that Coaching can do that.

I believe that we live in a world where holding hands and learning from each other is soon becoming the norm. It is the only way in which we will be able to move forward. It is the only way in which we will learn, together, to truly Be. To be in love with our lives and to honour our potential. To find deep and lasting fulfilment. To share our richness and our beauty with everyone else, in joy. You can do it! See you there!

* * * *

Silvana is a successful Inspirational Coach, philosopher, writer and teacher.

More than anything else Silvana is a passionate human being driven by a deep commitment to create a better, happier world for everyone. She founded Life Coaching with Silvana to reach out and make her own contribution through empowering individuals to embrace and fulfil their potential, follow their dreams and live life with joy and gratitude. Silvana currently lives in the UK and divides her time between writing, coaching, group coaching, teaching, travelling, supporting humanitarian projects and conducting workshops and seminars.

To get in touch with Silvana, to know more about her Coaching practice, her projects and the events she organizes visit www.LifeCoachingWithSilvana. com

To get her book "Being You and Loving You – The Ultimate Guide To Fulfilment" together with free materials and more insights into the topic of fulfilment visit: www.LifeCoachingWithSilvana.com

Your Life Energy

AMAL INDI

I have 20 years of experience in the tech sector and corporate banking. In my previous life in the "Rat Race", I was waking up every day and going to a job that provided well for me. After some major changes in my life (including a divorce), I started recognizing that I wasn't intrinsically happy. I would be going about my day filled with negative thoughts and emotions. It felt as though they were taking over in a way, and I recognized how they were beginning to affect every moment of my day and every interaction with those around me. I refer to these as "Thought Bugs", which I will go on to explain later. These Thought Bugs were almost like a computer virus, affecting all the thoughts or, as one may say, programming in my mind. After recognizing these Bugs and studying them in myself for many years, I began to draw strong conclusions about how I could create positive change in my mind. This positive change in my thoughts would eventually lead to me leaving the "Rat Race" and starting on the mission of my life to share my new paradigm with those around me. I believe that we can change our minds and create a positive and uplifting life, not only for ourselves, but for those around us. I would love to share with you the basics of what I discovered, a new way of examining our thought patterns and how to drastically shift the energy around you (your Aura) so that you can lead a fantastic life!

GETTING STARTED ON YOUR OWN JOURNEY

When was the last time you really felt 100%? When I say 100%, I mean you wake up feeling a general positivity in your mood, you are looking forward to a new day, your interactions with people feel good, and you walk around feeling a general sense of purpose even with the simple tasks of getting groceries or whatever your work environment. You may think that you have no say in how you really feel. That deep down, you cannot control your thoughts and emotions. I know that this is not true. I developed a unique way of seeing our minds and how deeply they affect our energy. Have you heard of life energy, such as positive energy, negative energy, Aura energy, and universal energy? Read on!

WHAT MAKES US HUMAN?

Each one of us is a biological marvel of different cells, tissues, genes. These are the many working pieces that come together to create our human body. What really makes us human in a whole sense? We each possess an in-depth energetic landscape that we can't deny. This energetic pulse is used by scientists and technicians daily to perform tests and create pictures of our bodies and their functions. Think of the neuroscientists that connect our bodies to electrodes and measure our brain waves. That's part of it. We can't deny there is a part of us beyond just the tissues of our muscles and bones.

Did you know that surrounding you right now is an energy field that is all your own? This energetic field is referred to as your Aura. This Aura can be the beginning of a life that you love. Every human being has an energy field around them. We cannot see this field with the naked eye. However, we can see this field with an Aura machine. It's true! I personally have had mine captured and what was reflected back to me (in terms of energetic levels) was what I was truly feeling.

Your Aura and the energy you radiate is 100% in your control. Some days, you might feel positive and good, while other days, you may feel more negative and lower. These are your energy levels. They can vibrate high or low. It depends on you and your thoughts. Remember, with improvements to your mind and thoughts, your aura energy field will continuously change, thus altering the life you are leading.

YOUR AURA

Over the centuries of humans existing and contemplating our existence, many have acknowledged the fact that we have an energy that extends beyond our skin and flesh, which can actually interact with the world around us. This is referred to as your body's Aura. The Aura refers to the energy around your body that can be affected from the inside out or the outside in. When it is strong, the Aura around your body can extend quite a way beyond the barrier of your physical body (your skin). It can also manifest as different colours, depending on the emotional mood of the person. For example, when you are

163

in a state of calm, then you will exude a white Aura. When you are in a state of anger, then you will exude a red Aura. Sometimes Auras may also be a combination of different colours. There is technology now that can show the colour and strength of someone's Aura. I have had mine checked. One day, it was light in colour and extended far beyond my body. This didn't surprise me as I feel I live in a state of calm, clear energy and my inner emotional landscape is positive. If you were to have an opportunity to get yours checked today what do you think the results would be? Strong and white? Or weak and maybe red? Maybe you feel like it may not show up at all.

This is what I want to teach you. This is my mission right now: To help you understand that you can empower yourself and create a strong, positive Aura that will not only affect your overall sense of well-being. It will affect your relationships, your business, and your life as a whole.

YOUR HUMAN SYSTEM

Through my own exploration, I began seeing and noticing a pattern in how my Aura was being affected by different things in my life. As I continued to study this in myself, it became clear to me that that there were specific things in play, and it was all rooted in my mind. Having a strong background in technology, I began to clearly see how our own minds behave like supercomputers. (Stay with me here!) Just like a super computer, we have our own operating system and the ability to run many programs at once. We are constantly juggling responsibilities, taking in the world around us, assessing how we feel, and determining what we need. The list could go on and on! Just take a moment right now: close your eyes and connect to all the "programs" open in your mind that are constantly running. Relate that to being connected to your own unique operating system of your mind. Now imagine that a computer virus was implanted into one of your programs and began affecting your thoughts. Computer viruses are designed to spread to all parts of a computer with the goal of eventually changing the computer, more often than not, making it completely dysfunctional. This is what can happen in your mind. A negative thought may enter your mind about something specific. Maybe a co-worker engages you in conversation about a rumour that someone is up for raise (one that you applied for) or on your coffee break the barista makes a mistake on your order and you feel it ruins your morning. I call these viruses of our thoughts Human Errors. In its most basic form, Human Errors can be outlined as the following emotions, or what I like to call Thought Bugs:

- Anger
- Suspicion
- Craving
- Comparison
- Low self-esteem
- Procrastination
- Getting stuck in negative thoughts

What it can be boiled down to is that these negative thought bugs can enter into your mind, which in turn creates negative energy. This leads to stress and a weakening of your Aura.

I'm sure you can think of a definitive moment, probably even within the last day or the last week, where you can see how your own errors were affecting your core system and negatively impacting the energy around you.

Luckily, we have a set of more positive emotions and various ways of reacting that counter the negative ones. I have identified these and aptly named them our Human Features.

Primary Human features that combat the errors include:

- Love and kindness
- Acceptance
- Forgiveness
- Courageousness
- Patience
- Authenticity
- Gratefulness

One can think of these features as a built-in tool box to combat negativity. This is always at our disposal! I want to help you identify where these positive emotions are in you, so that you may have access them and strengthen the energy that you are putting out into the world and your Aura.

Look, I am not a psychologist. I am not a therapist. I am, however, a believer in how we show up to our work and interact with those around us will have a deep impact on the life we are creating for ourselves. I have firsthand experience. I have taken myself from a place of negativity and darkness to a place of possibility. I have watched my newfound passions and work flourish, along with my relationships, personal and otherwise.

This is a different way of looking at things. This just isn't your usual "Be positive" message. This is connecting into the fact that as humans, we have a distinct design in place to help us truly create a good life for ourselves. The foundation of this is to truly feel happy and positive from the inside out, so that what we engage with is affected by our positive energy. Think of the last time you had an encounter with someone who you felt emitted a positive or happy energy? How did it make you feel? How did you react? You truly have the power to combat these negative thought processes (bugs) already in you! Don't you want to be the one truly living in your potential and sharing your positivity with everyone and everything in your life?

THE "AWESOME LIFE" IS WAITING FOR YOU!

Let's get down to business. Thanks for sticking with me. If you have continued reading to this point, then I want to applaud you! It means that you are deeply interested in living your best life.

Side effects of a mind free from negative Thought Bugs may include:
- General feelings of happiness and relaxation
- Genuine connections when meeting people
- A mind free from clutter
- A deep appreciation for the world and people around you
- High levels of productivity
- Willingness to learn new skills
- Gaining more contacts and connections with ease
- Feeling an authentic excitement for projects and self-development
- Being ready to rock your life!

These are just a few of the feelings available to you if you commit to removing negative Thought Bugs from your life, thus strengthening your energy and Aura from the inside out. I wouldn't be here today if I didn't do the work and experience the benefits of being on the other side of the process.

BRING LIGHT TO YOU

My hope for you is to learn how to identify your negative Thought Bugs and stop their process of multiplication. For you to empower yourself with positivity and strengthen your aura. For you to leave feelings of depletion behind and bring your energy back to 100%. For you to share your positive energy with the world and make it a better place!

Never forget: An Awesome Life is within your reach at all times. I believe it. In fact, I will go so far as to say I know it is. I have taken my own life and made it awesome by taking all I have outlined in my work and applying it to myself. Now it is your turn to turn up the positivity in your life and let your Aura shine!

I encourage you to check out my website, www.happinessmountain.com, to receive a free guide on removing your negative energy. In this guide, you will also be given a sneak peek into the app I am developing. The Happiness Mountain™ app will quickly become your new best friend! I developed the Happiness Mountain™ app to be a way to actually track those negative Thought Bugs and coach you to clear your worries and boost your energy levels! By giving you this important tool at your fingertips, I know you will be able to strengthen your energy and basically start living a more happy life! If you haven't guessed already, I love technology and its possibilities for enhancing our lives. I can't wait for you to be one of the first people to try this app and reap its benefits right away at www.happinessmountain.com/app.

BRINGING LIGHT TO YOU SO THAT YOU MAY BRING LIGHT TO THE WORLD

Now that I have given you some insight on how you can truly change your life by changing your own energy, I want to share the ways that Happiness Mountain™ can help you begin to apply these concepts. The process of understanding, application, and execution is key when committing to changing the way your mind functions and, over time, changing your aura.

Now that you know you have the power to change your life via your thoughts, I wonder why you wouldn't want to act now to change your life. Your own personal idea of an awesome life is within reach! I left behind an old way of living and being in order to start on a new path. I am confident that you have the power to do that for yourself as well. We all just need a little help. To be honest, I wish I had connected with these deeper levels of understanding regarding my thoughts and how they affect my life earlier. However, as we all know, timing is everything, especially when it comes to your advancement on both a personal level and a business one. Take this as a sign that it may be time for you to dive into these deep changes. The techniques, once you really begin to understand them, are quite straightforward. I know that you live a busy life and are striving to do your best. However, it takes commitment to change. Why not start now?

Happiness Mountain™ can offer you many tools to get started and help you dive deeper. The first step is easy! I encourage you to head over to my website www.happinessmountain.com to sign up and stay connected to the developments in my work. You will automatically receive an easy to follow guide on how to remove your negative energy, which will be delivered right to your inbox! You will also be given an automatic sneak peek into my app.

THE HAPPINESS MOUNTAIN™ APP

I am constantly inspired by how we connect online through different platforms and technologies. I believe that this can be the start to a great change in how we grow and develop. I designed the app as a convenient way for you to connect to your energy boosting practices on the go. We all spend some time on our phones scrolling and engaging on different platforms. Why not invest that time mindfully instead of mindlessly? The Happiness Mountain™ app, www.happinessmountain.com/app, helps you do that by having the tools you can utilize to boost your own positive energy available at any time!

Features include the following:

- Troubleshooting what is worrying you and replacing that worry with positivity

- Ways to resolve disputes without creating negative energy and affecting your Aura

- Aura boosting activities you can do on daily basis, while tracking your progress with your own private point system

- An emergency toolkit for handling sudden negative situations

- An easy guide to all the Thought Bugs and how to handle them available at a touch of your screen, so that you may continue to learn how you can change your thoughts to more positive ones and keep your positive energy high!

HAPPINESS MOUNTAIN™ FOR KIDS

Calling all parents and anyone who takes care of children! This work isn't just applicable to more mature minds and bodies. It can start when we are young! I am in the process of finishing development on a series of books for children that will cover all the core concepts of my work and Happiness Mountain™, so that we may share these valuable tools and concepts even with the developing minds of the next generation. Of course, there will be interactive games for children as well, because as we all know that some of the best learning happens when we are having fun! This goes for adults too, don't you think? Stay in the loop by connecting with me at www.happinessmountain.com.

MY NEXT BOOK

I am ready to dive deeper and share with you even more in my new book, *Happiness Mountain™: Double Your Happiness, Awesomeness and Spirituality*. In the book we are going to explore deeper than ever before. *Happiness Mountain™* will go more in depth on how you can harness the three levels of energy (Positive/Negative, Aura and Universal) to change your perspective and unlock your perfect life. I want to share with you the techniques and deep processes that will affect all aspects of your life. Remember those 'Negative Thought Bugs' I was talking about earlier? In my new book I will teach you not only how to eliminate them, I want to teach you how to protect yourself from future encounters with 'Negative Thought Bugs' therefore truly creating change in your life for the better. You will also learn techniques on how to recharge your energy, boost your aura and use your new skills for resolving conflicts and affecting your business.

I want you to harness the power of your personal Positive & Aura energies, learn to dance with the Universal energy that is always at your disposable and be able to live at a level of existence that falls in line with your ideal, perfect life. Take a look at the *Happiness Mountain™* diagram on the next page. You can define your perfect life as living with a high level of inner peace, the level of inner happiness. Your Awesome Life and Spiritual Life revolves around being of service to others and helping others. You can live a combination of all levels of the *Happiness Mountain™*. Whatever you personally define as perfection is where you have the power.

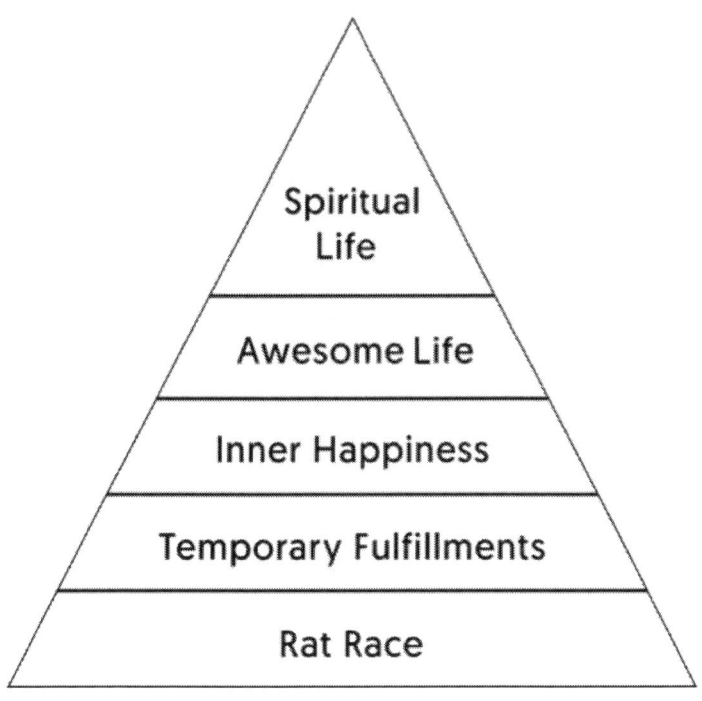

Happiness Mountain^{TM} created by Amal Indi

Some might argue you cannot have a perfect life. I say you already have a perfect life and it is blocked by negative energy from coming into full fruition. This negative energy can be existing as a low self-esteem bug or a comparison bug. You may define perfect life as comparing to others. You may try to achieve things with craving energy. Please remember: You are already whole, complete and perfect. You cannot access your full power because of the negative energy being generated by your thoughts. When you learn to remove those negative thoughts as I teach you in *Happiness Mountain^{TM}*, you will realize how much power you have in life. This will be your turning point to harness the energy to power-up your personal, business and spiritual life! In the book I will give you all the tools and techniques to accomplish that. After reading my new book *Happiness Mountain^{TM}* you will be able to shift your life to a new paradigm that is not only accessible but exciting. How do you think it will feel to lead a perfect life? Can you think of even one thing that may change for the better if you decided to investigate how you could crush your negative energies, enhance your positive energies and essentially eliminate future worries from your life? ... Wow! I am excited for you just thinking about it myself! I know the profound changes it created for me in my life and I look forward to hearing how it affects yours.

YOU CAN LEAD AN AWESOME LIFE

My hope for you is to learn how to identify your negative Thought Bugs and stop their process of multiplication. For you to empower yourself with positivity and strengthen your aura. For you to leave feelings of depletion behind and bring your energy back to 100%. For you to share your positive energy with the world and make it a better place!

Never forget: The Awesome Life is within your reach at all times. I believe it. In fact, I will go as so far to say I know it is. I have taken my own life and made it perfect in my eyes by taking all I have outlined in my work and applying it to myself. Again, your negative thoughts may say your life is not perfect, which might include your low self-esteem, cravings, or comparison bugs blocking you. Don't let these bugs create negative energy. Instead, clear them and power-up the personal, business, or spiritual aspects of your life. Never forget you have the power over your own mind- NOT your negative Thought Bugs. Now it is time to power-up the positivity in your life and let your Aura shine!

I encourage you to check out my website, www.happinessmountain.com, for the opportunity to stay connected to the global community of people who have already begun to use this work to boost their positivity and create their

Awesome Life in their personal, business, and spiritual domains. I can't wait for you to begin using The Happiness Mountain™ App to start training your energy to stay positive and even get stronger. Of course, I encourage you to visit www.happinessmountain.com to stay connected and be in the know as to what is coming down the pipeline with this life changing work.

I have dedicated my life to bringing these concepts and work to you. I know you can change your energy and begin to not only affect your own life, but the entire world. I believe deeply that when as many people as possible align their energy to a higher, more positive state, then we can truly make a collective difference. Let's start today!

Amal Indi lives in Vancouver, Canada, and is the founder and CEO of Happiness Mountain™ Inc. After 20 years of working in technology and corporate banking, Amal is on a mission to give people the possibility to live with their full potential in their personal, business, and spiritual domains. He has found innovative techniques and tools to remove negative energy and power up your personal life, business life, and spiritual life. Ultimately, you can make the world a more awesome place for everyone. He believes that technology has the potential to transform the minds and energy of people and facilitate change. Amal wants to help people around the globe live a positive and enriching life through the energy-based tools and techniques of this innovative system he has developed to strengthen your energy and help you live a life full of happiness and potential. Find his story and work at www.happinessmountain.com.

46963945R00105

Printed in Poland
by Amazon Fulfillment
Poland Sp. z o.o., Wrocław